Keeping and Improving Today's School Leaders

Keeping and Improving Today's School Leaders

Retaining and Sustaining the Best

Edited by
Bruce S. Cooper and
Sharon Conley

ROWMAN & LITTLEFIELD EDUCATION
A division of
ROWMAN & LITTLEFIELD PUBLISHERS, INC.
Lanham • New York • Toronto • Plymouth, UK

Published by Rowman & Littlefield Education
A division of Rowman & Littlefield Publishers, Inc.
A wholly owned subsidiary of The Rowman & Littlefield Publishing Group, Inc.
4501 Forbes Boulevard, Suite 200, Lanham, Maryland 20706
http://www.rowmaneducation.com

Estover Road,
Plymouth PL6 7PY,
United Kingdom

British Library Cataloguing in Publication Information Available

Library of Congress Cataloging-in-Publication Data

Cooper, Bruce S.
 Keeping and improving today's school leaders : retaining and sustaining the best / Bruce S. Cooper and Sharon Conley.
 p. cm.
 Includes bibliographical references.
 ISBN 978-1-60709-963-5 (cloth : alk. paper) — ISBN 978-1-60709-964-2 (pbk. : alk. paper) — ISBN 978-1-60709-965-9 (electronic)
 1. School management and organization—United States. 2. School administrators—Training of—United States. 3. Educational leadership—United States. I. Conley, Sharon C. II. Title.
 LB2805.C6314 2010
 371.2'011—dc22   2010029286

∞™ The paper used in this publication meets the minimum requirements of American National Standard for Information Sciences—Permanence of Paper for Printed Library Materials, ANSI/NISO Z39.48-1992.

Printed in the United States of America

Contents

Foreword

Michelle D. Young

A small but growing body of evidence suggests that school leaders play a pivotal role in the school improvement process (Hallinger & Heck, 1996; Leithwood & Jantzi, 2000; Robinson, Lloyd, & Rowe, 2008). School level leadership influences school culture, teachers' perception of their work environment, and the quality of the teaching staff. For example, effective schools research over the past 30 years indicates that principals who could hire and retain high-quality teachers were key to effective schools (Papa, Lankford, & Wyckoff, 2002). Similarly, Brewer (1993) linked higher student outcomes to schools with larger portions of the teaching team hired by principals with high standards, and Strauss (2003) concluded that principals can affect student achievement through the teacher hiring process.

Research also suggests that principals must remain in a school for a number of consecutive years to fully impact a school. Given the importance of educational leadership and the stability of quality leaders, the current rates of leadership turnover in many schools across the United States are troubling, making volumes like Cooper and Conley's *Keeping and Improving Today's Educational Leaders: Retaining and Sustaining the Best* welcome resources.

Among the reasons why keeping and improving tomorrow's leaders is important, three are particularly noteworthy. First, principal and teacher retention are inextricably linked. Schools with high levels of principal retention tend to have higher levels of teacher retention, which can have serious negative or positive financial and educational impacts on schools. Second, any school reform effort is reliant on the efforts of a principal to support a common school vision that focuses on implementing and sustaining the reform effort over multiple years. Such efforts are clearly derailed with the turnover of a principal. Research, in fact, suggests that principals must be in place at least five years for the full implementation of a large-scale change effort.

Third, as with teacher turnover, there are financial costs to principal turnover. Not only does a school district have to spend resources on recruiting, hiring, and training a new principal but also the district's investment in the professional development of the prior principal is largely lost. One large urban district in Texas that recently lost over 50% of the secondary school principals hired a full-time recruiter to focus solely on identifying candidates to replace principals who leave the district.

Little systematic research has been conducted regarding the career paths and turnover of school leaders. The majority of research that has been conducted relied on data from small-scale survey research, case studies, and anecdotal evidence (e.g., ERS, 1998; Bell & Chase, 1993; Lunenberg & Ornstein, 1991). Moreover, most of this research focuses on tracking the routes that principals take from their teaching positions to their leadership positions and, to a lesser extent, documents the reasons individual leaders made certain types of career path decisions (Young & McLeod, 2001). For example, with respect to entering the principalship, we know that teachers decide within the first seven years of their careers to become administrators (Fuller, Young, & Orr, 2007), that female principals have more teaching experience and are older than male principals (Riehl & Byrd, 1997), and that males are more likely to become principals than females (Fuller, Young, & Orr, 2007; Papa et al., 2002).

Even with this increased interest in the careers of principals, our understanding of career paths is still relatively limited. Little is known, for example, about the mobility of leaders once in the profession. One study conducted by Papa et al. (2002) on principal career paths in New York found that approximately two-thirds of new principals leave the school in which they started their careers within the first six years, and that urban schools are much more likely to have less experienced principals and principals who received their bachelor's degrees from lower ranked colleges.

Although these researchers did not collect data on what motivates these leaders' departures, they did trace them to their new schools: many transferred within the same district and/or moved to schools similar to those they left. Such differences in experience and career movement may be directly related to capacities of schools to recruit and retain teachers, enact school reforms, and create a stable school culture.

According to a RAND (2004) study, turnover rates of school leaders in North Carolina and Illinois hover around 14 to 18% per year. Tracing school leaders in New York State public schools, as noted, Papa et al. (2002) found that approximately two-thirds of new principals leave the school in which they started their careers within the first six years. Using New York data as well, Papa (2004) found that as student enrollment increases, the likelihood of principal turnover grows. Fuller, Young, and Baker (in press) found that in Texas, 50% of building leaders left the principalship within three years and 70% quit within five years. Similarly, according to Fuller and Young's (2008) research on principal retention in Texas, principal tenure and retention rates vary dramatically across school levels, with elementary schools having the longest tenure and greatest retention rates and high schools having the shortest and lowest retention rates.

Moreover, these authors found that the school's level of student achievement in the principal's first year of employment heavily influenced principals' retention rates, with the lowest achieving schools having the shortest tenure and lowest retention rates and the highest achieving schools having the longest tenure and highest retention rates.

The percentage of economically disadvantaged students in a school also has a strong influence on principals' tenure and retention rates, with high-poverty schools having shorter tenure and lower retention rates than low-poverty schools; retention is somewhat lower in schools in rural and small town districts, and somewhat higher in suburban districts where students tend to be White and not economically disadvantaged (Fuller & Young, 2008).

Despite the insight provided by the aforementioned research, far too little research is available on the career paths of principals. Indeed, less is known about why leaders leave their schools at such alarming rates, what their working conditions are like, and what might enable districts to retain high-quality leaders more effectively.

The contribution made to this literature by this Cooper and Conley volume is thus noteworthy. Contributors to this book provide desperately needed insight into (1) the socialization of educational leaders, (2) the role of mentoring and professional development in the improvement and retention of leaders, as well as (3) the significance of administrative teams and district support for effective school leadership. Contributors also provide essential insight into the working conditions and challenges facing our school leaders today. The volume brings together some of the latest research and thinking on how to retain and improve educational leaders. And as such this research serves as a "just in time," high-quality resource for the field and the nation's schools.

REFERENCES

Baker, B. D., & Cooper, B. S. (2005). Do principals with stronger academic backgrounds hire better teachers? *Educational Administration Quarterly, 41,* 449–452.

Baker, B. D., Orr, M. T., & Young, M. D. (2007). Academic drift, institutional production and professional distribution of graduate degrees in educational administration. *Educational Administration Quarterly, 43*(3), 279–318.

Ballou, D. (1996). Do public schools hire the best applicants? *The Quarterly Journal of Economics, 111*(1), 97–113.

Bell, C., & Chase, S. (1993). The under representation of women in school leadership. In C. Marshall (Ed.), *The new politics of race and gender* (pp. 141–154). London: The Falmer Press.

Boyd, D., Lankford, H., Loeb, S., & Wyckoff, J. (2005). The draw of home: How teachers' preferences for proximity disadvantage urban schools. *Journal of Policy Analysis and Management, 24*(1), 113–132.

Brewer, D. J. (1993). Principals and student outcomes: Evidence from U.S. high schools. *Economics of Education Review, 12*(4), 281–292.

Educational Research Services. (1998). Is there a shortage of qualified candidates for openings in the principalship? Arlington, VA: National Association of Elementary School Principals and National Association of Secondary School Principals.

Fuller, E., & Young, M. D. (2008). The revolving door: Principal turnover in Texas. *Texas Study of Secondary Education, 17*(2), 14–19.

Fuller, E., Young, M. D., & Baker, B. (in press). The relationship between principal attributes, school-level teacher quality and turnover, and student achievement. *Educational Administration Quarterly.*

Fuller, E., Young, M. D., & Orr, M. T. (2007, April). Careers in motion: An examination of the career paths of principals in Texas. Paper presented at the annual meeting of the American Educational Research Association. Chicago, IL.

Hallinger, P., & Heck, R. (1996). Reassessing the principal's role in school effectiveness: A review of empirical research, 1980–1995. *Educational Administration Quarterly, 32*(1), 5–44.

Leithwood, K., & Jantzi, D. (2000). The effects of transformational leadership on organizational conditions and student engagement with school. *Journal of Educational Administration, 38*(2), 112–129.

Lunenberg, F., & Ornstein, A. (1991). *Educational administration: Concepts and practices.* Belmont, CA: Wadsworth Publishing Company.

Papa, Frank C. Jr., Lankford, H., & Wyckoff, J. (2002). *The attributes and career paths of principals: Implications for improving policy.* Albany, NY: University of Albany, SUNY.

Papa, F. (2004). *The career paths and retention of principals in New York State.* Submitted to the University of Albany, State University of New York in partial fulfillment of the requirements for the Degree of Doctor of Philosophy. Albany, NY.

RAND. (2004). *The careers of public school administrators.* Research Brief: RAND Education. Santa Monica, CA.

Riehl, C., & Byrd, M. A. (1997). Gender differences among new recruits to school administration: Cautionary footnotes to an optimistic tale. *Educational Evaluation and Policy Analysis, 19*, 45–64.

Robinson, V. M. J., Lloyd, C. A., & Rowe, K. J. (2008). The impact of leadership on student outcomes: An analysis of the differential effects of leadership types. *Educational Administration Quarterly, 44*(5), 635–674.

Strauss, R. P. (2003). *The preparation and selection of public school.* A paper for the 28th conference of the American Educational Finance Association. Orlando, FL.

Young, M. D., & McLeod, S. (2001). Flukes, opportunities and planned interventions: Factors affecting women's decisions to enter educational administration. *Educational Administration Quarterly, 37*(4), 430–462.

Chapter One

Keeping Today's Educational Leaders

Sharon Conley and Bruce S. Cooper

School leaders, teachers, staff—and parents—are all concerned about getting and keeping the best leaders for their schools. This book tells them how: what to do (and not to do) to accomplish these goals. In particular, the book characterizes the qualities of approaches to school management, administrator socialization, and career development for supporting school leaders and retaining them in the education profession.

The book looks at the features of administrator professional development practices, administrator-teacher relationships, use of resources, changing work environments, and new models of school organization that are promising in sustaining and retaining the best leaders for U.S. schools. As Berliner (2007) emphasized, schools are essentially human enterprises, and the cultivation and retention of critical personnel who staff them are paramount.

Who is responsible for ensuring positive school management, human development and capacity building, and change? How are school improvement and change accomplished? In what ways can the leadership of both administrators and teachers be nourished? How can educators stimulate growth in a system that examines and takes into account school culture, community, and educational experience?

To address these questions, this book takes a broad, eclectic approach, bringing together a range of scholars examining leadership socialization, activities, growth, and effectiveness. Crow (1990) posed the question of what motivates site leaders to carry out their weighty responsibilities, asking, "Is it less important to understand the incentives of instructional leaders than to understand what motivates teachers?" (p. 38). Indeed, he noted that if we can identify those aspects of administrators' work that encourage them to remain in the profession, district and state policy makers will have a basis for redesigning job components and creating incentives that retain and recruit effective site leaders.

Site and district leaders perform difficult and complex work, and the incumbents in these positions deserve closer attention and help. In addition, universities and other preparation programs need a deeper understanding of what works. Therefore, this book brings together some of the latest research and practices to *sustain and keep* administrators in U.S. schools. As we know from years of research, leadership is important to figuring out what's working or not working, and thus what needs changing, and how best to proceed.

This book is part of a two-part series. The first book in the series, *Finding, Preparing, and Supporting School Leaders: Critical Issues, Useful Solutions*, focused on two major trends: (1) understanding leader preparation and adjustment to new roles and (2) understanding leaders' career attitudes and aspirations (Conley & Cooper, 2011). With regard to the former, the book addressed the move toward the growing standardization of the background and education of administrators who are recruited to schools and described contemporary methods of maintaining standards and improving training for the next generation of leaders.

Because school leaders continue to adjust and change throughout the administrator life cycle, also examined was the leadership "pipeline" (the pathway into the principalship and superintendency—usually "flowing" from the classroom to the assistant principal's office to the top jobs in the school and district). With regard to the latter, topics examined were whether administrative positions were effective and satisfying and how key interactions and relationships affected these leaders and their decisions to seek promotion in the administrative career—or not.

This second volume brings into focus the need to keep tomorrow's educational leaders by helping to retain and sustain them in their positions. We analyze the mentoring and renewal process for school leaders and what we know about getting that second chance of leadership. What can we do to make the principalship and superintendency more attractive posts and improve access to them? What can we do better to renew and support those already in those positions, to mentor minority leaders, and to support diversity? What do new developments in organizational theory and school management imply for growing and sustaining tomorrow's leaders?

This book is an essential resource for future leaders, education faculty in universities, professional associations, school district leaders, board members, and others interested in preparing and providing in-service education for the 200,000-plus leaders of American schools and school systems.

Like its companion volume, what we can learn from the perspectives and examples presented in this book will help in many ways: (1) to improve the nature of professional preparation, support, and mentoring needed to sustain our leaders; (2) to focus planning of in-service activities for working school administrators at all levels; (3) to help leaders throughout their careers do a better job; and (4) importantly, to keep the flow of new leaders coming, as they go from teaching to transitioning from assistant principal to principal, to ascending to the central office, to considering the superintendency and remaining there. And researchers of the education profession and/or leadership development will want to read this book, as it has implications for human and professional development, now and into the future.

THE PROBLEM

School leaders, at the school site and district levels, have never had an easy job. With dwindling funds and resources, coupled with tougher state and federal standards and fatigue from more regulations and testing, many school administrators are giving up—or crashing and leaving their posts. As in our first volume, we continue to reflect on Richard O. Carlson's (1969) finding several years ago that organizations in need of change are more likely to look outside their borders for new talent, while schools and districts that are working well may wish to promote from within.

But in focusing on these career and work orientations, Carlson doesn't examine in depth the organizational career development and qualities of good recruiting, reviewing, responding, renewing, and rewarding that could lead to better levels of support and retention. We again present Mulvey and Cooper's (2009) Six R's of good professional development and support. In our book (Conley & Cooper, 2011), the Six R's were adapted from teacher to administrative careers: leading from Recruitment to Retention, *with the critical Four R's in between*: Reviewing, Renewing, Responding, and Rewarding. Presently, the Six R's are being applied to leadership support as we seek to build and hold on to new leaders in our schools and districts (see Figure 1.1).

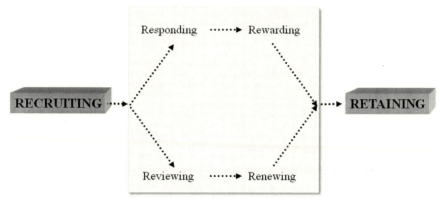

Figure 1.1. Six R's of New Teacher Retention: Conceptual Framework for Retaining Quality Personnel

New school leaders are often asked to administer the more challenging schools, such as those identified as chronically low performing in urban, suburban, and rural locations. In New York City, for example, Trachtman and Cooper (2011) described the difficulties of low-performing schools, staffed in part by teachers placed on "fast tracks" for certification. Principals, who often had a hand in hiring these personnel and who were also charged with their orientation and socialization, faced a high turnover of these new teachers early in the principals' tenures, even when the number of teacher recruits was initially encouraging.

Trachtman and Cooper (2011) recommended that principals become more readily available, master teachers in their own right, and teacher mentors helping to recruit and retain them in the profession. Change-of-career (midcareer) candidates or older personnel reentering the workplace in such settings also required new modes of management from principals (Marinell, 2011). Myriad challenges were faced by principals amid their striving to meet academic standards driven by No Child Left Behind (NCLB), as well as responding to the needs of increasingly diversified student populations, demonstrating a commitment to equity for all students (Petersen, 2011; Trachtman & Cooper, 2011).

Recognizing the complicated problems faced by school and district leaders, this book begins with the Six R's model (previously described) to examine the process of encouraging and retaining quality leaders at the school and district levels. This model suggests that the process of keeping new administrators charged with providing critical organizational supports (Guskey, 2000) follows these six steps:

Step 1—*Recruiting and Preparing* New School and District Leaders: With shortages in many districts, schools and districts need to pay attention to finding quality administrators, providing them with "realistic" job previews (Wanous, 1973), and ensuring a match between the administrative job, the school, and the leader. Step 6—*Retaining* these Administrators: We need to track the careers of administrators, from preparation to advancement through the administrative ranks, finding ways to help administrators be successful with teachers at different stages of their careers.

The four intervening steps are important and comprise much of this book's focus, leading to retaining administrators in the profession by helping to ensure that administrators are adjusting to their work and being sustained by their leadership positions.

Step 2—*Responding*: This step involves the role of the district and school leadership in focusing on and responding to the needs of education leaders as they take on and are socialized into their posts, and includes ideas related to Job Satisfaction (feeling the job generally meets expectations) and Growth Satisfaction (feeling the job is an outlet for further growth and development) (Conley, Shaw, & Glasman, 2007; Hackman & Oldham, 1980).

Step 3—*Reviewing and Understanding:* Leaders' needs and growth regularly are regarded as critical to new school improvement (Crow, 2007). Feedback is the key: not critical or threatening, but coming from administrative superiors and/or mentors showing understanding and being helpful.

Yet as the role of school leaders becomes more complex, so too does the difficulty of reviewing and understanding leaders' needs. For example, structural reforms such as charter schooling, decentralizing, and school choice may blend traditional roles in very specific patterns for each leader (Glasman & Heck, 2003; Smylie & Crowson, 1993). Reviews should include discussions about individual performance, group (team) performance, as well as opportunities for improved work design and further career development; that is, features of principals' jobs that focus on immediate opportunities to work on "meaningful" tasks or which career paths might provide a more continuous sense of career progression over time.

Finally, Step 4—*Rewarding and Recognizing:* This has been shown to be important for administrators throughout their careers (Marshall & Kasten, 1994). Distinct periods of time in the careers of site leaders include trainee, intern, assistant principal, novice principal, and experienced principal (Glasman & Glasman, 2007). Administrators may focus on different undertakings at different times, such as opportunities to exercise autonomous decision making and to facilitate collaborative work with others for novices—and serve as an exemplary model "while working on conflict" and develop "a greater love of people, learning, and teaching" for experienced administrators (Glasman & Glasman, 2007, pp. 136, 154).

In addition to financial compensation, providing leaders much-needed recognition for their accomplishments, helping them to communicate what they are doing to other administrators (colleagues and superiors in the administrative hierarchy), and reaching out to teachers, parents, and their communities are key steps in sustaining and retaining them (Crowson & Morris, 1985).

And to ensure that administrators won't necessarily quit, give up, or find another position, *Retaining* (Step 6) continued leadership requires a *Renewal* (Step 5) of spirit, knowledge, and growth—giving feedback and more time for reflection (Bolman & Deal, 2008; Collinson & Cook, 2007).

THE CHAPTERS

In Chapter 2, "Socialization of Assistant Principals," Ernestine K. Enomoto uses qualitative methods to explore a rural school district and its professional development. The chapter analyzes how the rural district conducted professional development for its assistant principals (APs), while considering the professional and organizational socialization literature related to leader preparation.

In Chapter 3, "Administrative Teams," Sharon Conley and Margaret Christensen examine quantitative survey data from principals and assistant principals in a region of one western state to learn about their perceptions of the administrative teams. What are the characteristics of administrative teams (e.g., task autonomy, team coordination) that could be enhanced to contribute to renewing and appreciating school leaders? As the concept of "distributed leadership" suggests (Spillane, 2001), leadership comes not from a single individual but from shared participation and governance.

In Chapter 4, "Leading in Financially Stressful Times," Rick Ginsberg and Karen D. Multon maintain that leaders often face difficult decisions that in turn have an emotional impact on them, with leaders being unprepared for the stress and confusion. The chapter explores the impact of leading, particularly at a time of high-stakes accountability and shrinking budgets. What are the implications for improving leaders' jobs, as well as leaders' abilities to cope with the challenges faced?

In Chapter 5, "Routines, Rituals, and Revival," Sharon Conley, Terrence E. Deal, and Ernestine K. Enomoto emphasize that school leaders entering new job assignments often act to alter routines, those everyday patterns of behavior that persist in schools. These leaders are changing "routines," but they are also changing rituals. Both routines and rituals can and do create opportunities for revival and the organization's preservation of well-established traditions.

In Chapter 6, "Mentoring Latina/Latino Leaders," Kenneth R. Magdaleno looks at rationales for creating an administrator mentoring system for Latina and Latino leaders to address issues of equity, access, and effectiveness. He finds that the close Latino/Latina community was a strong base for supporting new school leaders and being models for teachers and families.

In Chapter 7, "Leadership for Superintendents Leading Principals," Robert Roelle and Bruce S. Cooper apply quantitative methods to explore the significance of the relationship between superintendents' leadership practices using the *Five Practices of Exemplary Leadership* defined by Kouzes and Posner (2008), and principals' job satisfaction, efficacy, and career longevity, as reported by principals themselves.

Finally, in the Epilogue, "Retaining and Sustaining the Best in a Dynamic Environment," Rick Ginsberg provides a summation of this book's chapters, identifies pertinent themes, and offers additional insights about what can be done to get and keep better (and more) school leaders in these challenging times.

This book, then, offers a perspective on renewing educational leaders as they deal with the many challenges faced in American public schools. Beginning with a chapter on a case study of leadership socialization and concluding with a study of exemplary leadership practices for district administrators, the various chapters offer contemporary views on aspects of sustaining and retaining school administrators. As such, they provide insight into what should and must be done to reinvigorate and keep the best leaders within U.S. schools.

REFERENCES

Berliner, D. C. (2007). Foreword. In A. B. Danzig, K. M. Borman, B. A. Jones, & W. F. Wright (Eds.), *Learner-centered leadership: Research, policy, and practice* (pp. xi–xiv). Mahwah, NJ: Lawrence Erlbaum.

Bolman, L. G., & Deal, T. E. (2008). *Reframing organizations: Artistry, choice, and leadership.* San Francisco: Jossey-Bass.

Carlson, R. O. (1969). *Career and place bound school superintendents: Some psychological differences. A project report.* Eugene, OR: Eugene Center for Advanced Study of Educational Administration.

Collinson, V., & Cook, T. F. (2007). *Organizational learning: Improving learning, teaching and leading in schools and school systems.* Thousand Oaks, CA: Sage.

Conley, S., & Cooper, B. S. (2011). *Finding, Preparing, and Supporting School Leaders: Critical Issues, Useful Solutions.* Lanham, MD: Rowman & Littlefield Education.

Conley, S., Shaw, S., & Glasman, N. (2007). Correlates of job and professional satisfaction among secondary school administrators. *Journal of School Leadership, 17*(1), 54–88.

Crow, G. M. (1990). Perceived career incentives of suburban elementary school principals. *Journal of Educational Administration, 28*(1), 38–52.

Crow, G. M. (2007). The professional and organizational socialization of new English headteachers in school reform contexts. *Educational Management Administration and Leadership, 35*(1), 51–71.

Crowson, R. L., & Morris, V. C. (1985). Administrative control in large-city school systems: An investigation in Chicago. *Educational Administration Quarterly, 21*(4), 51–70.

Glasman, N. S., & Heck, R. H. (2003). Principal evaluation in the United States. In T. Kellaghan and D. L. Stufflebeam (Eds.), *International handbook of educational evaluation* (pp. 43–59). Dordrecht, Holland: Kluwer Academic Publishers.

Glasman, N. S., & Glasman, L. D. (2007). *The expert school leader: Accelerating accountability.* Lanham, MD: Rowman & Littlefield.

Guskey, T. (2000). *Evaluating professional development.* Thousand Oaks, CA: Corwin Press.

Hackman, J. R., & Oldham, G. R. (1980). *Work redesign.* Reading, MA: Addison-Wesley.

Kouzes, J., & Posner, B. (2008). *The leadership challenge* (4th ed.) [electronic version]. San Francisco: Jossey-Bass. Accessed online at Books24x7.

Marinell, W. H. (2010). Midcareer teachers and tomorrow's leaders. In S. Conley and B. S. Cooper (Eds.), *Finding, Preparing, and Supporting School Leaders: Critical Issues, Useful Solutions*. Lanham, MD: Rowman & Littlefield Education.

Marshall, C., & Kasten, K. L. (1994). *The administrative career: A casebook on entry, equity, and endurance*. Thousand Oaks, CA: Corwin Press.

Mulvey, J. D., & Cooper, B. S. (2009). *Getting and keeping new teachers: Six essential steps from recruitment to retention*. Lanham, MD: Rowman & Littlefield.

Petersen, G. J. (2011). Superintendent leadership. In S. Conley and B. S. Cooper (Eds.), *Finding, Preparing, and Supporting School Leaders: Critical Issues, Useful Solutions*. Lanham, MD: Rowman & Littlefield Education.

Smylie, M., & Crowson, R. (1993). Principal assessment under restructured governance. *Peabody Journal of Education, 68*(2), 64–84.

Spillane, J. (2001). Investigating school leadership practice: A distributed perspective. *Educational Researcher 30*(3), 23–28.

Trachtman, R., & Cooper, B. S. (2011). Teaching principals to be master teachers, again. In S. Conley and B. S. Cooper (Eds.), *Finding, Preparing, and Supporting School Leaders: Critical Issues, Useful Solutions*. Lanham, MD: Rowman & Littlefield Education.

Wanous, J. P. (1973). Effects of a realistic job preview on job acceptance, job attitudes, and job survival. *Journal of Applied Psychology 58*, 327–32.

Chapter Two

Socialization of Assistant Principals

Ernestine K. Enomoto

This qualitative study explores how a rural school district, serving nine schools in three communities, provided leadership preparation for its assistant principals (APs). Over a school year, the researcher, together with district personnel, delivered administrator development sessions and conducted participant observations of the new leaders in training. Data were collected on meetings, classroom observations, and school visits in School Year (SY) 2005–2006. Findings present how the organizational socialization of new APs was accomplished and how these individuals responded as independent agents. Rural school leadership succession is also explored. Discussion considers what might make professional development less consistent than desirable to sustain new administrators in remote school settings.

INTRODUCTION

School leadership has been identified as one of the most important factors associated with effective, high-performing, and successful schools. However, principals and APs face numerous challenges in achieving those objectives. First, with current standards and accountability intensified by No Child Left Behind (NCLB), principals are directed to make changes and sustain school reform to achieve standards (U.S. Department of Education, 2002). Second, their student populations are increasing and diversifying with more families becoming economically disadvantaged, children identified as having specific learning needs, and students of limited English proficiency needing more assistance.

Meeting these kinds of challenges requires that school leaders be both knowledgeable and committed to equity for all (Marshall & Oliva, 2010; Scheurich &

Skrla, 2003). Third, school leaders are challenged with having to manage re-source allocations and often must defend their resources as well as seek alternative funding sources (Cunningham & Cordeiro, 2009). Finally, a shortage of qualified and trained school administrators is occurring at all levels (elementary, middle, high schools) and in all types of districts (urban, suburban, and rural) (Fink & Brayman, 2006; Quinn, 2002; Young, Petersen, & Short, 2002).

The problem of effective school leadership is especially challenging in hard-to-staff rural schools. According to Arnold (2004), one of every six school-age students lives in a community of less than 2,500 residents. Not only must rural school leaders find qualified teachers and provide sufficient resources to deliver education, but also they might face potential school con-solidations, closures, and a declining economic base for their communities (Barley & Beesley, 2007).

The scope of rural school leaders' work is often much broader than in other districts and includes economic as well as social implications for their small, remote communities. That said, the research studies on rural education, and particularly the literature on recruiting and retaining capable school leaders, have been sparse (Arnold, 2005; Arnold, Newman, Gaddy, & Dean, 2005; Browne-Ferrigno & Allen, 2006).

With the need for better school leadership especially in rural areas, how are new administrators being prepared? What are rural school districts doing to orient, educate, and socialize new leaders? What considerations are given to leadership preparation and succession in remote rural areas? This study of school leadership explores how one rural school district approached adminis-trator preparation and development, specifically for the APs in rural settings.

CONCEPTUAL AND CONTEXTUAL FRAMEWORKS

The study employed both organizational socialization and leadership preparation as conceptual frameworks to understand better how rural school leaders were being prepared in this district. These two areas of research framed exploring the school district to train, support, and retain its new administrators. In addition, existing research on rural education school leader preparation was reviewed. This literature enabled a better understanding of the many challenges faced by leaders as well as important components to meeting those challenges.

Organizational Socialization

Literature on organizational socialization was used to examine the profes-sional development employed in work settings (Crow, 2006, 2007; Heck,

1995; Parkay, Currie, & Rhodes, 1992; Stevenson, 2006). By definition, socialization refers to how individuals break from the past and learn new roles within the organization (Jones, 1986). This process is especially useful in considering how veteran teachers might approach becoming and succeeding as school administrators. They begin to internalize the values, beliefs, and norms of the new group, eventually becoming part of it (Browne-Ferrigno & Muth, 2004; Hart, 1991, 1993; Leithwood, Steinbach, & Begley, 1992). Learning what is expected, individual leaders become more competent in their work, more satisfied, and thus more likely to remain on the job (Falcione & Wilson, 1988; Lester, 1987; Morrison, 1993).

Additionally, individuals were found to interpret rather than simply respond to their work roles, suggesting that socialization is bidirectional and dynamic rather than presuming that only the organization acts in the process (Crow & Matthews, 1998; Saks & Ashforth, 1997). Taking this into account, the interaction between individuals and organization was examined in this study and used to describe the socialization of new administrators, many of whom had spent years within the same school or rural district.

Leadership Preparation and Succession

Leadership preparation often begins with transitioning from teacher to department head or curriculum coordinator and culminates in formal university training and licensure to become an educational administrator (Cunningham & Cordeiro, 2009). Findings have shown a gap between what is learned in formal preparation and what is needed for principals to succeed in their schools (Walker & Qian, 2006). Traditional university preparation for educational administrators has been critiqued as the profession becomes more complex and the challenges in schools more demanding (Howley, Andrianaivo, & Perry, 2005). Crow (2006) suggests that traditional preparation programs are far from adequate and proposes a need for more conceptual understanding of socialization in line with the dynamic and complex work of a school administrator.

Once appointed, many school leaders receive little more than a building map and set of keys. Their induction into the profession is more often "sink or swim socialization" (Hart, 1993). According to Draper and McMichael (2000), new principals have felt abandoned in the first years, as they might only receive attention when problems occur. Already anxious and frustrated over their new roles, beginning principals might have to fit into an existing school culture and battle the "ghosts of principals past" (Walker & Qian, 2006, p. 301).

Hargreaves and Goodson (2006) found that "leadership successions were always emotionally intense events" (p. 18), citing that teachers mourned the loss of charismatic leaders and expressed worries over new replacements. Teachers might not accept new leadership and change (Ogawa, 1991) and could resist or ignore those "revolving door" principals (Macmillan, 2000). With the responsibility clearly placed on the leadership, beginning principals tend to feel isolated, overwhelmed, and overworked.

RURAL SCHOOL LEADERSHIP PREPARATION

Compared with their counterparts in urban and suburban regions, beginning principals in rural schools have greater professional development needs (Howley, Chadwick, & Howley, 2002). They tend to have less education, are more geographically isolated from peers, have a wider range of role responsibilities, and have higher turnover rates. According to Arnold et al. (2005), "being a rural administrator is a difficult job that fewer and fewer people are willing to take" (p. 18).

In a rural early career principal academy in Ohio, features such as mentoring and networking through small study groups were found to be valuable components to mitigate the effects of geographic isolation (Howley, Chadwick, & Howley, 2002). Similarly, Peterson and Kelley (2001) found that networking was possible through interdistrict collaborations, distance-learning technologies, and summer institutes.

Also important was setting high expectations for school leaders, as noted by district administrators' reflections about the professional development initiated for principals in rural Kentucky (Browne-Ferrigno & Allen, 2006). Recognizing the rural district's needs and challenges, superintendents and their leadership teams reframed the expectations of their principals from that of school managers to instructional leaders. Through a joint university-district collaboration, they reenvisioned educational leadership with different role and work expectations for school principals. They recruited principals who would "both make a difference with students and make a commitment to stay in Pike County" (p. 7). Intensive professional development—delivered over time, job embedded, and reflective—made this leadership shift possible.

This study sought to determine how one rural school district actually delivered its professional development and demonstrated a commitment to preparing new school APs. What was the educational organization doing to ensure that these individuals knew the roles, responsibilities, and expectations of their work as school leaders? How were these APs being groomed to become the heads of their respective rural schools and communities?

How were the individuals responding and reacting as novice administrators who had also been veteran teachers in one school? Were they "inexperienced and unprepared administrators left to manage" or was there succession planning and systematic socialization into the profession, especially in rural communities?

Qualitative Research Methods

To explore these questions, the study employed a qualitative research approach (Merriam, 2001, 2002; Stake, 1995; Yin, 2003). The primary participants were the eight APs in the leadership development program. Key informants included their respective principals, the district superintendent, and a consultant-mentor who worked with the leadership during the school year.

While planning meetings began the spring beforehand, data were primarily collected over a school year, based upon participant observations at 18 on-site administrator meetings, 11 days of classroom visits to different schools, and 13 planning meetings with the superintendent and others. The data included field notes of observations, photographs of groups, seating arrangements, interview transcripts, and documents relevant to the school district such as policies, procedures, newspaper articles during the time, and website information on all of the schools.

Since the intent of the research was primarily to examine how socialization occurred in the field, participants were observed as they interacted and constructed their understandings about leadership development. Rather than generating propositions ahead of time, inductive reasoning was used in examining the professional development shaping these educational leaders as they learned their roles and responsibilities in the school district. The phenomenon of professional development was considered as it was evolving in the field (Bogdan & Biklen, 2007; Wolcott, 1994).

The following steps were employed in conducting the study. First, I identified the natural setting, a rural school district where the researcher could be part of the leadership development process and spend considerable time in the field. I was able to spend a school year's time beginning in the summer of 2005 and concluding in spring 2006. The purpose of being in the district was to assist in the leadership development process of school principals and APs in the school district. Specifically, I was a direct participant in planning, organizing, and delivering sessions for the assistant principals' group. Additionally, the superintendent conducted monthly school principal meetings and visitations of schools and classrooms in the district.

The second step was identifying the participants in the study, primarily the eight APs for the schools in the district whose perspectives were the focus.

Other informants in the study included the school district superintendent, an adjunct consultant who served as a mentor for new principals, nine school principals, and several school resource personnel involved in leadership preparation at various times during the school year. As in most qualitative research studies, the sampling was purposive where the subjects of interest were the current leadership in the district's schools.

The third, fourth, and fifth steps were executed concurrently in collecting data, considering possible propositions about findings, and analyzing as well as synthesizing the data into descriptions of what seemed to be occurring. Through this iterative process, propositions were generated from the data to direct a closer scrutiny of the leadership preparation conducted in the district.

Periodically, field notes were checked with the consultant-mentor, and she was asked questions to validate or critique impressions, perceptions, and so on. By way of summative evaluation, a final report of overall impressions was delivered to the superintendent and consultant in a culminating meeting in spring 2006. Recommendations for consideration by the leadership in the school district were also given to the school administrators at a later time.

Because of my position as a university faculty member and consultant to the district, I was personally invested in making sure that the leadership sessions were designed and delivered in the best way possible under the direction of the district superintendent with a team of other presenters. Our preparatory sessions were collaborative and needed to be flexible. Observation and interview data were solicited and validated by talking with both the superintendent and the consultant-mentor. Through this means, researcher biases were kept in check.

In the next sections, the rural school district with its schools is first described and the professional development program as designed is presented. Following those descriptions, the findings are organized in terms of three research questions regarding organizational socialization and leadership preparation.

Rural School District ABC

Like many school districts across the country, the state of Hawaii's public education system was facing a leadership crisis, with the majority of its principals and assistants approaching retirement age and two-thirds of the current administrators being 52 years of age and older (Daniel, Enomoto, & Miller, 2003). Vacancies were common in 40% of the assistant principalships around the state, with those in rural and some urban pockets higher than in other areas. The recruitment and retention of administrators involved (a) identifying qualified staff members, (b) providing professional development opportunities that were both timely and relevant, and (c) linking training with successfully promoting students' educational achievement.

Organizationally, recruitment and retention of school level administrators are handled through a statewide system. Unique among the 50 U.S. states, Hawaii maintains a centralized public education system distributed over 15 school districts known as "complex areas." At the direction of an elected statewide school board, the state superintendent oversees all operations with the help of 15 complex area superintendents in charge of high schools and their respective feeder schools (i.e., elementary and middle grade levels). While the recruitment and professional development of new administrators are handled centrally by the state system, district superintendents are expected to hire, supervise, and support the administrators within their respective complex areas.

The ABC school district in this study served youngsters in three distinct communities in a sporadically populated area of the state (see Table 2.1). For confidentiality, pseudonyms were used for all areas, schools, and persons mentioned in this study. The first community, Able, was the most remote, located over 60 miles from the nearest micropolitan area (i.e., population of at least 10,000 but less than 50,000 residents).

It included two historic towns, one with a combined elementary and secondary school (grades K–12), and the other town with a K–7 school. Students at the elementary school would be bused to the adjacent town for their secondary schooling. According to school reporting for SY 2005–2006, a total of 860 students were enrolled in the two schools.

Baker, the second community, had four public schools (two elementary, one middle, and one high school) serving 2,662 students from small towns and villages in the area. Built in 1999, Baker High was the most newly constructed secondary school in the district. Eighty percent of the students commuted to school, many relying upon subsidized school bus service, being transported from as far as 22 miles away.

The third community, Charlie, well established with one rural township and several historic villages, had experienced changing demographics. Recent low-cost housing developments and economic opportunities generated a growth spurt, increasing the number of families and school-age children in the area. School reports on the two elementary schools and one secondary school (grades 7 to 12) indicated that total student enrollment was 1,699 for SY 2005–2006.

Despite some variances among the nine schools in the district, all nine would be considered high-needs rural schools. Diverse in student demographics, the rural schools served from 60 to 84% free or reduced-price lunch

Table 2.1. ABC Schools Reference: School Year 2005–2006 Reports

Community	Able		Baker				Charlie		
School	A-1	A-2	BE-1	BE-2	BM-3	BH-4	CE-1	CE-2	CH-3
Grades	K–12	K–7	K–5	K–5	6–8	9–12	K–6	K–6	7–12
Students	502	358	743	419	633	867	610	339	750
Free & reduced-price lunches	59.6%	76.3%	70.9%	83.8%	75.5%	57.6%	77.7%	74.3%	67.1%
Special needs	19.3%	18.2%	9.2%	9.3%	17.2%	24.9%	13.1%	10.9%	19.9%
ELL	15.7%	29.1%	14.1%	2.4%	3.6%	6.0%	9.3%	8.6%	5.9%
Native minority	42.2%	38.4%	42.1%	62.7%	41.8%	39.3%	51.3%	39.1%	42.1%
Teacher count	40.5	28	47	28	45	60.5	42.5	24	58.5
5+ years at school	11	13	34	19	25	23	15	14	31
Licensed teachers	34	24	46	25	41	50	33	23	43
Administration*	4	3	2	2	4	7	3	2	7
Librarians	1	1	1	0	1	1	1	1	1
Counselors	3	2	2.5	1	4	6	2	2	4.5
Number of principals in last 5 years	2	2	2	2	2	2	1	3	1

*Administration includes principals, assistant principals, student activity and student services coordinators, registrars, and athletic directors.

recipients, between 9 and 25% students with special needs, 2 to 29% with limited English, and 38 to 63% native minority students (SY 2005–2006 school reports). All the schools except two in the Charlie community had had at least two principals within the last five years. Table 2.1 displays the break-down of student demographics by schools.

PROFESSIONAL DEVELOPMENT
PROGRAM AND PARTICIPANTS

Initiated by area superintendent Regina Zane, the school district's profes-sional development program was designed and developed for in-service AP preparation, the first step toward becoming a school administrator. While initial discussions about the program began in spring 2005 prior to SY 2005–2006, the first actual planning meeting was held in October 2005. At that time, Ms. Zane, consultant-mentor Sonia Stephens, and I discussed a range of topics that participants were interested in as well as content we felt was needed for their training. Topics included curriculum development, discipline procedures, facilities management, inclusion, mediation and arbitration, han-dling of referrals, and student support services.

We considered how the program might be delivered over two or three years and agreed to develop the following skills in the participants: (a) become good investigators of problems, (b) be collaborative and communicate effectively with faculty, staff, and peers, (c) become continuous learners in their profes-sion, and (d) demonstrate leadership with vision and initiative. To foster these skills, each leadership preparation session would contain five aspects: (a) con-tent and information coupled with skill building, (b) application to academic standards, student support, and school systems, (c) opportunities to network with peers and others, (d) conversations with the principals who supervised their work, and (e) reflections and opportunities for feedback. After plans were made, monthly meeting dates were established and all but one meeting were held. The March 2006 meeting was canceled due to inclement weather.

Eight APs from the ABC school district participated in the program. Only six of the nine schools in the district were represented among the participants because secondary or combined schools usually had one or two APs and only one of the elementary schools had an AP. Of the APs, six were females (Ar-lene, Cecilia, Nanette, Olivia, Rochelle, Terri), and two were males (Norman, Roger). Four (Cecilia, Norman, Rochelle, Terri) were relatively new to admin-istration, serving temporarily and having not yet been certified by the state.

At the time, Terri and Norman were seeking certification and attending the assistant principals' academy organized by the state. Four APs (Arlene, Nanette,

Olivia, Roger) had been at their schools for some time, working up from the teacher ranks into administration. Of these four, two (Arlene, Nanette) were already fully certified as administrators to become APs. While Arlene seemed interested in becoming a principal, Nanette had more pressing personal matters and was not seeking a principal's position at that time.

FINDINGS

Three key research questions were posed in this study. The first question dealt with administrators' socialization and development. What was the school district doing to socialize new, and for the most part, inexperienced administrators? The second question related to individual agency and responsiveness. How were these individuals responding and reacting as newcomers but also as veteran educators? The third question broadly asked about leadership succession connected with professional development. To what extent was organizational socialization effective or beneficial in securing leaders and retaining them, particularly in rural school settings?

Research Question 1: Professional Development Designed and Sometimes Delivered

In assessing how the school district was socializing its newest members, professional development was found to be designed but not delivered as anticipated. While formal sessions were organized and the superintendent was committed to preparing these APs, numerous interruptions prevented delivery of the scheduled program.

First, the superintendent was often called away for more pressing matters. For example, during the school year, incidents occurred such as a weekend fire at a high school, vandalism at the middle school, a gun incident/firearms violation, and a fight involving a nearby charter school. These incidents required Superintendent Zane's immediate attention, taking her away from the scheduled sessions with the APs. Other interruptions related to state responsibilities; for example, Regina was expected to be at the opening of the state legislature along with the other district superintendents. As she would need to spend the night in the state capital and fly back the next morning, Regina advised us to go ahead without her being present.

Usually after emergency incidents or events, Superintendent Zane would share what had happened, what procedures were in place (or not, as in the case of the weekend fire), and how decision making should occur at the school and district levels. Covering this information was important because she informed the administrators about district policies, procedures, and work responsibilities. Regina made clear what she was doing and how she managed the crisis. At the April meeting, for instance, she arrived in the afternoon with her resource teachers but received a phone call from the deputy superintendent to be briefed about the discipline policy and a recent gun incident that had occurred.

When "higher-ups" such as the deputy called, she needed to respond immediately. In the case of attending the legislature's opening session, she spoke about connecting with the specific legislators from ABC's three communities. While Regina often shared with the AP group, doing so meant that regularly scheduled topics would be postponed or preempted.

A second reason for alterations to the schedule related to presenters. Many of the guest speakers were from the state capital, and their scheduled visitation dates often changed. At the second meeting on December 9, the guest presenters were preempted because their boss, an assistant superintendent, had announced she was stepping down and staff needed to make changes accordingly. The announcement was made the morning of our meeting, altering the day's agenda.

In another case, the planning team had wanted to offer instruction on differentiated learning to accommodate diverse learners. However, no date could be arranged with the presenters, thus postponing the topic from one meeting to the next. These modifications in schedule were said to be like "changes in the wind" for which the ABC district would simply have to make do, adjusting its scheduling of events accordingly.

A third reason that changes occurred in professional development delivery related to the state system's proprietary place in leadership training for new school administrators. Although Superintendent Zane was committed to professional development and provided a unique hands-on style of leadership in her district, the state system had its own agenda, offering mandatory training sessions through its leadership academy. These sessions were required of all new principals and APs interested in certification. The academy also arranged and financed mentors to support new principals—Sonia Stephens, ABC's consultant-mentor, was one.

Understandably, the state system personnel felt that professional development sessions needed to be delivered consistently across the districts. Superintendent Zane appreciated the training and mentoring, but she commented privately that these sessions took time away from daily school operations, especially since administrators were required to leave their island communities to attend the sessions. Further, the information presented was often general, not directed toward immediate needs in specific schools in the ABC district.

Research Question 2: Individual Agency and Responsiveness

According to Saks and Ashforth (1997), individuals can and do act independently despite the directives of the organization; this was evident as not all APs completed their homework assignments as directed. For example, all were expected to make regular classroom visits and do at least 10 classroom observations within the month. This expectation was established at the first meeting in November. Superintendent Zane felt that professional development needed to be linked to observations and made a point to emphasize the importance of these regular classroom observations. In addition, the three of us (Regina, Sonia, and I) would be visiting the schools and joining with APs in doing classroom observations there.

However, by the third month, only three of the eight APs had completed all 10 classroom observations required in the month. Three other APs reported having done at least five. Superintendent Zane asked, "What have you learned? What has been happening as a result of your class observations? Are standards being implemented at the classroom level?" Some APs felt less comfortable doing the observations, as Norman told us during one of the observations at his school. Serving as a temporary AP at a high school, he was not familiar with secondary school curricula because he had been an elementary school teacher prior to his administrative appointment.

Other APs said that they were too busy with other responsibilities. For example, on the day we joined her for observations, Cecilia was on AP duty and could not participate in the debriefing after completing her classroom visits. Arranging for the time to do observations and debriefing about them was difficult for the APs to arrange.

By April, we were concerned that so few APs were doing the classroom observations and thus scaled back from 10 to 7 required each month. As if to explain why they were not doing these observations, the superintendent spoke about all the things that take up their time, like conducting special education meetings, managing personnel matters, handling student discipline, doing counseling, and other matters. In the end, the classroom observations expected of APs were not done at all. Thus, an important goal of the administrators' professional development was not accomplished.

Another example of individual action related to how APs viewed their attendance at these meetings. Often one or two APs were not present at meetings or might come and go during the daylong sessions. At the November meeting, for example, Nanette could only come later in the morning because she needed to be at her high school. Roger had a doctor's appointment and had to leave early from one AP meeting. Rochelle also needed to take her grandson to the doctor.

Occasionally, an AP would ask to leave before the 4:00 p.m. closing but more often they would slip out in the afternoon. Notably at one meeting, when Roger started to leave around 2:35 p.m., he was asked about directions to his school because he would be hosting the next gathering. He informed the group that he would send e-mail directions about driving and parking at his school. Rarely were individuals "called out" as Roger had been when leaving early. Later in private, the superintendent commented about the attendance issue, saying that principals should be making arrangements for their assistants to be attending trainings, not scheduling school meetings or requiring them to stay at school on professional development days.

Research Question 3: Linking Professional Development and Leadership Succession

Like the state superintendent, Ms. Zane addressed leadership succession with a commitment to professional development. Speaking directly to the administrators, she explained that "like funeral planning, you need to plan for who will be taking over your school." Its inevitability meant that the next generation of leaders would need to be trained. Directed toward that end, the centralized state system had initiated an "aspiring administrators" program to recruit new and potential leaders. It had also established a Principal's Academy to support and mentor newly appointed principals. Mandatory meetings had been planned, which at times were problematic because both the principal and AP might be out of school for an entire week of training.

In ABC district, Superintendent Zane expressed her commitment to providing support and training to her new administrators, the APs, as well as principals, by meeting regularly each month. Arrangements for the school year would be planned the spring before because the school year opened in late July rather than traditionally in September. The meeting dates for the principals were scheduled with separate dates for APs. Also, Regina was considering hosting meetings by communities, as for instance, having all Baker schools meet as a group once a month.

In terms of leadership changes occurring in the entire school district, two new elementary school principals were appointed the spring before. Both of them had been APs in secondary schools prior to their appointments. During the school year, Nathan, formerly a high school principal who worked in the central office, applied for and was appointed principal at one of Baker's elementary schools. Two principals were scheduled to retire; only one actually did retire that year. Roger, a seasoned AP, temporarily filled her position at Able's K–12 school. Unfortunately, Roger experienced health problems and did not want to be made principal at the school.

Another Able principal took a leave from her duties because of health problems, and her position was filled temporarily by Arlene, the certified AP. She had been a former special education teacher, serving for many years in both of the Able schools. Expressing an interest in becoming a principal, Arlene eventually was appointed to head Able's K–12 school, replacing its retired school administrator. Norman from Baker was temporarily appointed at Able's K–8 school and was later replaced with someone from out of the district.

Also changing roles were those in staff positions serving on Superintendent Zane's leadership team. Two resource personnel stepped down, one to take up doctoral studies and the other to retire. These leadership and staff vacancies presented challenges for the superintendent, who was often scrambling to find replacements, constitute search committees, and hire new personnel. For example, placing Nathan in a principalship meant that his position as personnel officer for the district would be vacant and might not be easily filled with a knowledgeable, qualified person.

DISCUSSION: CHANGES IN THE WIND

"Changes in the wind" seems an appropriate way to characterize the professional development delivered by this rural school district. Despite sincere efforts on the part of the superintendent and her leadership team, the findings in this study suggest organizational socialization at the district was not provided with the consistency and delivery to optimize best practices. Several explanations contribute to this outcome.

First, the rural district organization was a nested bureaucracy, more tightly coupled with its central statewide system and historically less connected to its schools. Superintendent Zane, while in charge in her own district, responded to her boss, the state superintendent; as such, whatever the state agenda established, she was obligated to carry out.

Also, the schools were nested within the district, so the APs responded to their immediate supervising principals, who apparently directed what was most important and urgent to learn and do at their respective schools. This nesting of school within district within state made for changes directed by the hierarchy; that is, APs responded to their principals, principals responded to Superintendent Zane, and ultimately she responded to her boss, the state superintendent.

The second reason relates to how individuals take the initiative and act as independent agents within an organization (Crow & Matthews, 1998; Saks & Ashforth, 1997). The socialization process attempts to change or modify that development; but in this study, findings suggest that the APs decided what was important, how to respond, and what actions were necessary. Notably at

the December 9 meeting, we spent considerable time talking about the process for making good decisions and how to determine what might be important as compared with urgent actions to take. That was helpful in clarifying
protocols and directing preferred or priority actions.

At the same time, four of the eight APs were more seasoned administrators,
having been at their school for a period of time. Their experiences made them
more inclined to take actions related to their schools or to take directives from
their immediate supervising principals than to follow through with requirements or expectations of the superintendent. The same could be said of two
recently assigned APs, who were expected to learn and be accountable to their
supervising school principal. One might speculate that the remote location
and resulting geographic isolation would reinforce this kind of action (Howley, Chadwick, & Howley, 2002).

A third explanation for the changes in the wind is the need for flexibility and
adaptability, given the challenges at the school, in the rural district, and in the
entire state. As reported in the findings, many events and incidents happened
in the course of the school year that required immediate attention, systematic
follow-up, and/or revised responses. Plans for professional development were
often revised on the day of the session because of more urgent school business
(e.g., discussing how to handle the fire that had occurred during off-school
hours), accommodating the schedule of guest speakers, unplanned absence of
the district superintendent, and other unexpected incidents.

On the one hand, changes in the wind might be thought of as flexibility on
the part of the district in delivering "just in time" and job-related types of
training (Browne-Ferrigno & Allen, 2006). On the other hand, these changes
could be viewed as an extension of crisis management with less control over
school information delivery and consistent socialization of leadership. Seeking a balance between flexibility and consistent delivery would be desirable
for sustaining professional development.

Finally, organization socialization presumes we know who is being prepared for what types of roles within the organization. We should consider that
leadership succession provides a focus on how the organization is identifying
the next generation of leaders and the roles they are expected to assume in the
organization. But this study suggests varied kinds of leadership roles and
changing needs within the school district.

For example, a principal vacancy might be filled by someone who creates
another vacancy, as personnel officer Nathan did when he applied for and was
appointed to be an elementary school principal. Also, a "revolving door" of
administrators might occur, as was the case at the two Able schools. Macmillan (2000) suggests that resistance to change by teachers and staff might
occur with frequent changes in administrators. A closer look at these kinds of

changes in leadership would be appropriate in considering leadership development for rural school districts.

IMPLICATIONS FOR RURAL SCHOOL LEADERSHIP

With a shortage of qualified and experienced school administrators particularly in rural areas of the country, professional development is critical if schools are to be improved and new leaders successful. This study provided an in-depth look at how professional development was planned, organized, and delivered based on how this rural school district attempted to socialize its new members, while considering the complexity of the organization delivering the leadership preparation with school, district, and state levels involved in socializing and supervising instruction.

Researchers might explore this further, as Crow (2006) suggests, by more closely examining the varied methods of socialization and perhaps even broadening traditional approaches beyond the particular school and educational organization. It might be useful to consider other social agencies like professional associations, community groups, religious organizations, businesses, and government agencies, because school leaders might provide the sharing, support, and integration among diverse groups in rural settings.

This study also indicated the dynamic, bidirectional nature of organizational socialization, taking into account that individuals can and do act independently. Following an individual's career path might be a useful way to understand a person's thinking, decision making, goals, and motivation in seeking to become a school leader. In this study, only one of the APs, Arlene, expressed a desire to move into the principalship, and she eventually did succeed in her goal. It would also be worth investigating why other individuals like Roger and Nanette chose to remain as APs and what might encourage them to consider becoming principals.

This study considered the linkages between professional development and leadership succession. Exploring them further might be done quantitatively to determine and measure consequences of professional development in building capacity and sustaining leaders. Changes in rural school leadership could be viewed over a longer period of time, such as five years or more, and perhaps with different models of leadership succession. For example, it might be appropriate to consider the dual role of teacher-administrator or a distributed leadership approach for rural schools (Arnold et al., 2005; Masumoto & Brown-Welty, 2009).

Finally, for those practitioners responsible for organizing and delivering professional development to prepare school leaders, the study suggested ways to think about what is being done, to whom, and to what end. As indicated by the findings, consistency was needed in delivery along with flexibility and responsibility. While it was appropriate to have planned sessions with the involvement of the superintendent, perhaps others like the APs might take on more leadership roles and responsibilities. This would accommodate the changes in schedule but still ensure consistency in content delivery over the yearlong program.

Further, as changes in leadership occur in positions other than the principalship, consideration might be more broadly conceived in planning for leadership succession linked with professional development and delivery. More can be done to ensure that professional development occurs to sustain school leaders in rural communities.

REFERENCES

Arnold, M. L. (2004). *Guiding rural schools and districts: A research agenda.* Aurora, CO: Mid-continent Research for Education and Learning.

Arnold, M. L. (2005). Rural education: A new perspective is needed at the U.S. Department of Education. *Journal of Research in Rural Education, 20*(3). Retrieved May 1, 2009 from http://jrre.psu.edu/articles/20-3.pdf

Arnold, M. L., Newman, J. H., Gaddy, B. G., & Dean, C. B. (2005). A look at the condition of rural education research: Setting a direction for future research. *Journal of Research in Rural Education, 20*(6). Retrieved December 18, 2009 from http://jrre.psu.edu/articles/20-6.pdf

Barley, Z. A., & Beesley, A. D. (2007). Rural school success: What can we learn? *Journal of Research in Rural Education, 22*(1), 1–16. Retrieved May 1, 2009 from http://jrre.psu.edu/articles/22-1.pdf

Bogdan, R. C., & Biklen, S. K. (2007). *Qualitative research for education: An introduction to theory and methods, 5th ed.* Boston: Pearson.

Browne-Ferrigno, T., & Allen, L. W. (2006). Preparing principals for high-need rural schools: A central office perspective about collaborative efforts to transform school leadership. *Journal of Research in Rural Education, 21*(1), 1–16. Retrieved May 1, 2009 from http://jrre.psu.edu/articles/21-1.pdf

Browne-Ferrigno, T., & Muth, R. (2004). Leadership mentoring in clinical practice: Role socialization, professional development, and capacity building. *Educational Administration Quarterly, 40*(4), 468–494.

Crow, G. M. (2006). Complexity and the beginning principal in the United States: Perspectives on socialization. *Journal of Educational Administration, 44*(4), 310–325.

Crow, G. M. (2007). The professional and organizational socialization of new English headteachers in school reform contexts. *Educational Management Administration & Leadership, 35*(1), 51–71.

Crow, G. M., & Matthews, L. J. (1998). *Finding one's way.* Thousand Oaks, CA: Corwin.

Cunningham, W. G., & Cordeiro, P. A. (2009). *Educational leadership: A problem-based approach (4th ed.)*. Boston: Pearson.

Daniel, S. J., Enomoto, E. K., & Miller, E. L. (2003). *Ventures in leadership: A strategic plan for addressing Hawaii's school leadership needs*. Honolulu, HI: University of Hawaii Press.

Draper, J., & McMichael, P. (2000). Contextualizing new leadership. *School Leadership and Management, 20*(4), 459–473.

Falcione, R. L., & Wilson, C. E. (1988). Socialization processes in organizations. In G. M. Goldhaber & G. A. Barnett (Eds.), *Handbook of organizational communication* (pp. 151–169). Norwood, NJ: Ablex.

Fink, D., & Brayman, C. (2006). School leadership succession and the challenges of change. *Educational Administration Quarterly, 42*(1), 62–89.

Hargreaves, A., & Goodson, I. (2006). Educational change over time? The sustainability and nonsustainability of three decades of secondary school change and continuity. *Educational Administration Quarterly, 42*(1), 3–41.

Hart, A. W. (1991). Leader succession and socialization: A synthesis. *Review of Educational Research, 61*(4), 451–474.

Hart, A. W. (1993). *Principal succession: Establishing leadership in schools*. New York: State University of New York Press.

Heck, R. H. (1995). Organizational and professional socialization: Its impact on the performance of new leaders. *The Urban Review, 27*(1), 31–49.

Howley, A., Andrianaivo, S., & Perry, J. (2005). The pain outweighs the gain: Why teachers don't want to become principals. *Teachers College Record, 107*(4), 757–782.

Howley, A., Chadwick, K., & Howley, C. (2002). Networking for the nuts and bolts: The ironies of professional development for rural principals. *Journal of Research in Rural Education, 17*(3), 171–187.

Jones, G. R. (1986). Socialization tactics, self-efficacy, and newcomers' adjustments to organizations. *Academy of Management Journal, 29*, 262–279.

Leithwood, K., Steinbach, R., & Begley, P. (1992). Socialization experiences: Becoming a principal in Canada. In F. W. Parkay & G. E. Hall (Eds.), *Becoming a principal: The challenges of beginning leadership* (pp. 284–307). Boston: Allyn & Bacon.

Lester, R. E. (1987). Organizational culture, uncertainty reduction, and the socialization of new organizational members. In S. Thomas (Ed.), *Culture and communication: Methodology, behavior, artifacts, and institutions* (pp. 105–113). Norwood, NJ: Ablex.

Macmillan, R. (2000). Leadership succession: Cultures of teaching and educational change. In N. Bascia & A. Hargreaves (Eds.), *The sharp edge of education change: Teaching, leading and the realities of reform* (pp. 52–71). London: Routledge & Falmer.

Marshall, C., & Oliva, M. (2010). *Leadership for social justice (2nd edition)*. Boston: Allyn & Bacon.

Masumoto M., & Brown-Welty, S. (2009). Case study of leadership practices and school-community interrelationships in high-performing, high-poverty, rural California high schools. *Journal of Research in Rural Education, 24*(9). Retrieved December 18, 2009 from http://jrre.psu.edu/articles/24-1.pdf

Merriam, S. (2001). *Qualitative research and case study applications in education.* San Francisco: Jossey-Bass.

Merriam, S. (2002). *Qualitative research in practice: Examples for discussion and analysis.* San Francisco: Jossey-Bass.

Morrison, E. W. (1993). Newcomer information seeking: Exploring types, modes, sources and outcomes. *Academy of Management Journal, 36,* 557–589.

Ogawa, R. T. (1991). Enchantment, disenchantment, and accommodation: How a faculty made sense of the succession of its principal. *Educational Administration Quarterly, 27*(1), 30–60.

Parkay, F. W., Currie, G. D., & Rhodes, J. W. (1992). Professional socialization: A longitudinal study of first time high school principals. *Educational Administration Quarterly, 28*(1), 43–75.

Peterson, K., & Kelley, C. (2001). Transforming school leadership. *Leadership, 303*(3), 8–11.

Quinn, T. (2002). *Succession planning: Start today.* Retrieved February 28, 2008 from the National Association of Secondary School Principals website, www.nassp.org

Saks, A. M., & Ashforth, B. E. (1997). Organizational socialization: Making sense of the past and present as a prologue for the future. *Journal of Vocational Behavior, 51,* 234–279.

Scheurich, J. J., & Skrla, L. (2003). *Leadership for equity and excellence: Creating high achievement classrooms, schools, and districts.* Thousand Oaks, CA: Corwin.

Stake, R. E. (1995). *The art of case study research.* Thousand Oaks, CA: Sage.

Stevenson, H. (2006). Moving towards, into, and through the principalship: Developing a framework for researching the career trajectories of school leaders, *Journal of Educational Administration, 44*(4), 408–20.

U.S. Department of Education. (2002). *No child left behind.* Washington, DC: Author.

Walker, A., & Qian, H. (2006). Beginning principals: Balancing at the top of the greasy pole. *Journal of Educational Administration, 44*(4), 297–309.

Wolcott, H. F. (1994). *Transforming qualitative data: Description, analysis, and interpretation.* Thousand Oaks, CA: Sage.

Yin, R. K. (2003). *Case study research: Designs and methods (3rd edition).* Thousand Oaks, CA: Sage.

Young, M. D., Petersen, G. T., & Short, P. M. (2002). The complexity of substantive reform: A call for interdependence among key stakeholders. *Educational Administration Quarterly, 38*(2), 137–175.

Chapter Three

Administrative Teams

Sharon Conley and Margaret Christensen

In the context of current and projected shortages of educational administrators nationwide, enhanced attention is directed by states and districts to how administrative jobs might be altered better to attract and retain site leaders in their positions (Educational Research Service [ERS], 2000). The major state administrative organization in California, for example, projected an approximately 40% turnover in the ranks of principals over a four-year period (2008–2012). This loss is caused primarily by principal retirements and/or movement to central office positions to replace retiring baby boomer superintendents (Association of California School Administrators [ACSA], 2008).

Despite current initiatives including administrator mentoring programs that aim to ease the transition of new recruits to principal, many potential applicants do not appear eager to enter site-leader positions. They may, for example, view administrative jobs as little more than "endless rounds of meetings and a call to nonstop problem solving" as opposed to opportunities to "make deep and lasting difference in instruction and learning and to develop leadership skills" (ACSA, 2008).

Therefore, once in their positions, administrators may experience low job satisfaction (Conley, Shaw, & Glasman, 2007; Eckman, 2004; Pounder & Merrill, 2001), which as Conley et al. pointed out, makes two work reactions more probable: psychological and physical withdrawal from the job (see also Beehr, 1995; Hulin, Roznowski, & Hachiya, 1985). Principals and assistant principals (APs) charged with bringing about school change (Fullan, 2007)—but who are less than fully engaged in their jobs—are likely to experience diminished interest in serving as school leaders. Thus, the shortage of principals is exacerbated (Cooley & Shen, 2003).

This chapter explores the design of effective *administrative work teams* as one potential avenue for increasing and assuring the continuous psychological and work engagement of school administrators. Our focus is at the high school level, where the administrative team typically consists of the principal, the AP or vice principal(s), and potentially other administrators such as the dean of students.

A substantial line of organizational behavior literature suggests that effectively designed work teams engage their members, finding ways for members to function together such that they experience high job satisfaction as well as increase members' intentions to stay in the organization (Hackman & Oldham, 1980; Hackman, 1982; Hackman, 1990). Because the effective design of administrative teams may be a potent contributor to the overall enhanced retention of the school leadership talent pool, this chapter examines team characteristics that contribute to perceptions of administrative team effectiveness.

RELATED LITERATURE

To improve understanding of administrators, their work, and their work teams, two areas of literature were examined. First, attention is directed to selected literature on administrators' work and current job challenges, examining the potential contribution of teams to alleviate such challenges. Second, literature on work group effectiveness is examined, in particular Hackman and Oldham's (1980) model (see also Hackman, 1990). This literature provides further understanding of the characteristics of administrative teams that may contribute to the enhanced quality of administrators' work experience on teams and administrative team effectiveness.

ADMINISTRATORS' WORK

High school administrators occupy visible and challenging positions with major responsibility. Although some might suggest that administrators' command of high salaries compensates for stressful work conditions, the position is nonetheless challenging and demanding. One illustration of the substantial time demands placed on high school administrators can be found in after-school activity supervision. Each Friday during the fall football season, it would not be unusual for many administrators at a comprehensive high school to perform their normal duties at school from 7:00 a.m. until as late as 5:00 p.m.

They might then return to the stadium early in the evening to supervise the activities of students attending the game. Once the game concludes, administrators may remain until the stands are cleared and students have left the area, possibly as late as 10:30 p.m., thus dedicating a 15.5-hour workday to their administrative jobs.

The demands illustrated by the above example appear consistent with a growing literature characterizing the work of principals and APs as both time-consuming and complex (Eckman, 2004; ERS, 2000; Fullan, 2007; Grubb & Flessa, 2006; Pounder & Merrill, 2001). The myriad of expectations for the principal include not only supervision of extracurricular activities but also managing issues of school violence and safety, leaders' complex relationships with department chairs, master schedule construction, and new strategies for teaching and learning (Conley et al., 2007, p. 55; Pounder & Merrill, 2001). Especially at the high school level (with many student bodies exceeding 2,000), Eckman found "unreasonable time demands and pressures on the principal" as well as the "perception among potential candidates that one must be a 'superman' to meet all of the expectations of the position" (p. 367).

In Eckman's (2004) study of "role conflict," role commitment, and job satisfaction among high school principals in three midwestern states, specific conflicts reported by administrators included "time for privacy, time for social commitments, meeting expectations for self, feelings of guilt and household management" (p. 377). Eckman suggested that these conflicts resulted from the "excessive time demands" of the positions as well as the conflict between personal and professional roles documented in much of the research (e.g., Vadella & Willower, as cited in Eckman, 2004, p. 370).

Further, an ERS (1998) study asked superintendents to identify what they believed most often prevented people from applying for the principalship. Superintendents delineated the following top three factors: "compensation insufficient compared to responsibilities," a job that is "too stressful," and "too much time required" by the position (cited in ERS, 2000, p. 26). This study suggests that high salary levels appear insufficient to match time and other demands.

In this context, effectively designed administrative teams may be one way of redressing the high demands of the position. For principals and APs charged with activity supervision and student discipline, administrators working in well-functioning teams might alleviate stressful conditions by dividing tasks differently (Grubb & Flessa, 2006). For newly recruited administrators, the informational and social support from strong administrative teams may be particularly valuable in providing them with the assistance they need to be successful (Campbell, 2001; Pellicer & Nemeth, 1980). And for administrators overall, to the extent that team members view their efforts as part of a team as opposed to an individual enterprise, they may be able to focus on tasks rather than spreading themselves too thin (Hackman & Oldham, 1980).

Schools with highly effective administrative teams would seem likely not only to encourage retention but also to create a positive managerial atmosphere for the school as a whole. However, little research has been conducted on administrative teams in education. This omission appears less than helpful in providing guidance to schools desirous of improving the way administrators work in their schools, likely enhancing the experiences of administrators as well as teachers, support staff, and students.

A focus on administrative teams also appears consistent with the concept of distributed leadership (Grubb & Flessa, 2006; Spillane, 2001), underscoring that leadership emerges from shared participation and governance as opposed to the efforts of a single individual.

WORK GROUP EFFECTIVENESS

To guide an investigation of the characteristics of administrative teams that work effectively and engage their members, Hackman and Oldham's (1980) *work group effectiveness* model is one of the most widely applied in studies of work teams. According to this model, administrative teams would be considered "work groups" for three reasons.

First, administrative work groups are *real groups*, or intact social systems, complete with boundaries (e.g., between administrative and teaching staff), interdependence among members, and differentiated member roles. Second, the teams have a *task* to perform, or an outcome for which members have collective responsibility, such as the effective administration and management of a school. Third, they operate in an *organizational context*; that is, they manage relations with other individuals or groups in the larger social system such as the district administration (Hackman, 1990).

Before identifying major aspects of team design and functioning posited to contribute to overall team effectiveness, it is necessary to specify what is meant by work group effectiveness. Work groups are effective, according to Hackman and Oldham (1980), if the group produces outcomes that are both high in quantity and quality; that is, enough work is produced that is sufficiently worthwhile. An additional aspect of work group effectiveness is the extent to which members are committed to their particular team and desire to continue participating on it.

Indeed, as a "high-involvement" strategy for improving human resource management, effective team design shares a critical commonality with participation, job enrichment, and workplace democracy strategies: the intention of empowering members and giving work more significance, thereby contributing to commitment and satisfaction (Bolman & Deal, 2003, p. 159).

Hackman and Oldham's (1980) model identifies four major contributors to work group effectiveness: design features, organizational support, task and interpersonal processes, and enabling conditions. First, initial or "setup" *design features* of the group refer to the design of the group task. These team-work features include a motivating structure for the group task, task autonomy, and skill complexity and are expected to motivate team members to high levels of performance. Furthermore, the team's composition—that is, its mix of individuals with their respective knowledge and skill—as well as its size (neither too large nor too small) are expected to enhance team effectiveness. Finally, group norms about interpersonal processes reflect an understanding of what behaviors are acceptable to the team during the conduct of its business.

Secondly, *organizational context* includes the rewards and objectives for good performance, availability of training and consultation, and clarification of task requirements and constraints. For example, in a business setting, a reward could be a team bonus; in an education setting, there might be special recognition of a high school administration team by the superintendent at a board meeting. In addition, charting new territory in a team task might require new information, skills, or knowledge; the organization might meet this requirement by providing opportunities for training and consultation.

Finally, teams require clarification of task requirements from the organization, such as deadlines, as well as knowledge of constraints, such as details on staffing limitations under which the teams must operate.

Thirdly, *task and interpersonal processes* include coordinating team actions and fostering commitment to the team's work; knowledge sharing and contributions of all team members; and implementing as well as inventing performance strategies in advance of accomplishing the task. One can envision that advance coordination, for example, could help reduce or eliminate unanticipated problems when the parties concerned (e.g., AP, dean of students) have had the opportunity to provide input and identify possible pitfalls, such as in master scheduling (Pellicer & Nemeth, 1980).

And finally, some related but conceptually distinct team characteristics, according to Hackman and Oldham (1980), are *enabling conditions* or intermediate criteria of work group effectiveness. These aspects focus primarily on behaviors of team members, notably the level of effort team members apply to team tasks, the appropriateness of the strategies the team uses to accomplish the tasks, and the amount of knowledge and skill the team applies to its work. Viewed as most closely related to how well a team ultimately accomplishes its task, enabling conditions can be expected to affect work group effectiveness directly (Hackman, 1982).

As noted, research on administrative work teams in education is scarce. However, research on *teacher* work teams that has utilized Hackman and Oldham's (1980) model provides insight into characteristics of shared work in school settings that might be relevant at the administrative level. Pounder and her colleagues (1999; Crow & Pounder, 2000) have carried out a series of studies on interdisciplinary teacher teams in middle schools over several years.

Their findings serve to illustrate some of the contributions of this research in identifying characteristics of effective teams. For example, Crow and Pounder's (2000) study of teacher teams in a suburban middle-level (grades 7 through 9) school reported that for some teams, scheduling constraints, often in the form of lack of block scheduling, were organizational context variables that inhibited teams' work. However, principal support, in the form of arranging "weekly release times" and providing teacher professional development, enhanced teaming efforts (p. 244).

An exception to the observation that administrative teams are overlooked in the literature is Grubb and Flessa's (2006) examination of the design of administrative teams with a focus on the coprincipalship. Although this study confined attention to alternative administrative structures—such as two principals, three principals, rotating principals, and a school with the principal's duties distributed among teachers—it yielded insights into characteristics of effective teams also highlighted in the broader team effectiveness literature.

In one K–6 school, for example, the responsibilities of a principal were divided among eight teachers sharing leadership. Among the benefits cited by coprincipals were the team's "modeling" and "working together" as well as the "beneficial" aspects of seeing team members interacting as "peers" (p. 533). To take another example, at this school and others in the study, leadership teams coordinated staff meetings so that coprincipals were "splitting the presentation of issues and plans, sharing the management of teacher comments, and clarifying their joint roles" (p. 533).

These observations are consistent with elements in Hackman and Oldham's (1980) model, such as viewing the work of the leadership team as a collective as opposed to individual enterprise and fostering commitment through the joint development of task performance strategies.

Thus, in exploring administrative work teams, we wanted to examine administrators' descriptions of the teams they are on in terms of characteristics suggested by Hackman and Oldham's (1980) model. Although the model has been useful in examining the perceptions of educators, such as middle school teachers participating on interdisciplinary teams (e.g., Crow & Pounder, 2000), it has not been generally utilized to examine the work of administrative teams. We hoped that a correlational study would provide considerations for altering the design of administrative teams in schools in ways that enhance the work experiences of administrators, including the quality of work and their commitment to their work teams.

SURVEY METHOD

A survey method explored administrators' perceptions of their teams, utilizing data from a small sample of medium-size school districts initially collected in 2002 from APs and principals in a California region, reanalyzing it to more closely explore some propositions in the model (for a fuller description of this study see Christensen, 2002). Secondary data analysis is a common practice in the social sciences, providing for more robust analysis (Babbie, 1973).

In addition, our selection of perceptual measures allowed us to place primary emphasis on individual administrators' *evaluation* of the extent to which design of teams, organizational support for teams, and interpersonal processes in teams sufficiently met expectations as opposed to the *objective* levels of these features (Bauer & Bogotch, 2001).

The study used survey data to operationalize and examine relationships among aspects of design features, organizational support, task and interpersonal processes, and enabling conditions (independent variables) and components of work group effectiveness (dependent variables) in Hackman and Oldham's (1980) model.

Sample and Data Collection

Eight school districts in central California with one or more comprehensive high schools were initially chosen for participation in this study. The districts were situated reasonably close to each other, were located in suburban or rural areas, and were geographically accessible, within 100 miles of the research team's location. District administrators (superintendent or assistant superintendent) were contacted by telephone or e-mail and asked if they would be willing to permit the comprehensive high school administrators to participate in the study. Five districts agreed to be part of the study. Surveys along with letters explaining the study and requesting participation were mailed to each high school administrator within the comprehensive high schools of the five districts.

Seventy-seven administrators (principals and APs) returned the survey. Of these, one survey was excluded from the sample owing to incomplete information. Therefore, the final sample size was 76, approximately 73% of the original sample. Of those administrators included in the study, 72% were APs or deans and 24% were in principal positions (2.7% were in other administrative positions and 1.3% did not respond to the question). In addition, over two-thirds (69%) of the respondents were male and 29% were female (2% did not report gender).

The sample was also fairly experienced, with 64% having 10 or more years of service in their current district. One-half of respondents indicated that it was unlikely they would leave their current positions, although just under one-third (28%) indicated that if they did leave, they would be likely or very likely to take another position in administration. Eighty-eight percent of the administrators reported that they planned to remain in the field of education in some capacity.

Instrumentation

Administrators reported information about the teams they were on, including how often they formally convened with team members,[1] and answered items tapping several of the research constructs (design features, organizational context, task and interpersonal processes, enabling conditions, and work group effectiveness). A primary source of items we utilized for the study was Conley, Fauske, and Pounder's (2004) adaptation of survey items and findings from Crow and Pounder (2000) and Hackman and Oldham (1980), as well as Hackman (1982).

ANALYSIS

This section describes the factor analysis. The following section describes the study variables classified by design features, organizational support, task and interpersonal processes, enabling conditions, and work group effectiveness. Most items were measured on a six-point scale ranging from 6 (strongly agree) to 1 (strongly disagree).

To explore the structure of the survey data, an exploratory factor analysis was conducted on the survey items.[2] Eighteen factors were identified. From these factors, 14 were selected as those most consistent with model concepts. A reliability analysis (Cronbach's alpha estimates) revealed that eight of the nine factors with multiple items had alpha coefficients of .69 or higher, suggesting high reliability; and for another factor the Cronbach's alpha was lower, indicating moderately low reliability (.59). The factor analysis suggested that several of the constructs from Hackman and Oldham's (1980) model were the appropriate ones, with one or more factors corresponding to, for example, design features, organizational support, enabling conditions, or work group effectiveness. In addition, some factors blended different aspects of the model; for instance, organizational support items pertaining to rewards, recognition, and task requirements and constraints loaded on a single factor rather than separately.

Further, a second factor combined some aspects of what Hackman and Oldham (1980) consider task and interpersonal process inputs (i.e., those related to fostering commitment, weighing inputs, and task strategies) with what they term enabling conditions (i.e., those related to effort and performance strategy). This factor primarily reflects an enabling condition but also addresses fostering commitment on the team.

STUDY VARIABLES

Design Features

Design features included the *motivational structure of the task*; *group composition (size, mix)*; *task autonomy*; and *skill complexity*. The motivational structure of the task was measured by a single item: "We clearly are a TEAM of people with a shared task to perform—not a collection of individuals who have their own particular jobs to do."

Group composition-size was measured by two items: "Our administrative team is the right size to do our work well" and "The size of our administrative team is (1 = too small, 2 = about right, 3 = too large)." Because the items used different response categories, the following recoding of the second item was performed (1 = too small, recoded to 2; 2 = about right, recoded to 5; 3 = too large, recoded to 2). Group composition-mix was measured by the following item: "Our administrative team has the right mix of people needed to do our job well."

Task autonomy described the level of authority team members had to manage their own work and the extent of initiative and judgment exercised by the team, and was composed of three items. Two sample items are "Our administrative team merely carries out work; the principal decides what is to be done and how it is to be done" (values reversed for coding) and "Our team has the authority to manage our work pretty much the way we want to."

Skill complexity described the extent of high-level skills required by the team's work and was measured as follows: "Members of our administrative team must use a number of complex and high-level skills to get our work done."

Organizational Support

Organizational support was tapped by a single variable, which described the overall level of rewards and recognition team members believed they received for good performance as well as the availability of training/consultation and information about task requirements. It was measured by six items. Sample items include "The district goes out of its way to show appreciation for especially good performance by our administration team" and "If our team needs some training or technical consultation to deal with a work-related problem, it is readily available to us."

Task and Interpersonal Processes

Task and interpersonal processes were composed of two variables, *coordination of team/group norms* and *knowledgeable team*. Coordination of team/group norms described the quality of communication and coordination behavior on the team and the presence of norms guiding interpersonal processes for conducting the work. It was composed of four items. Sample items are "Sometimes coordinating my work with other team members is more trouble than it's worth" (item reversed for coding) and "Our administrative team has clear standards for the behavior of administrative team members."

Knowledgeable team captured the extent to which team members possessed expertise or requisite knowledge for doing the team's work, as follows: "People in our team share their special knowledge with one another" and "Some people in our administrative team do not have enough knowledge or skill to do their part of the group task" (item reversed for coding).

Enabling Conditions

Enabling conditions dealt with the degree to which members applied sufficient effort, skills, and performance strategies to the team's work, and it was composed of three variables: *negative conditions, enabling condition–team quality,* and *enabling condition–contributing knowledge.*

Negative conditions described the extent to which team members perceived that *more* effort and knowledge/skill could be brought to bear on the team's work. It was measured by the following two items: "Our team could put substantially more effort into our work than we do at present" and "Our team could bring more knowledge and skill to bear on the group task than we do at present."

Enabling condition–team quality described the extent to which the team did foster commitment, create appropriate performance strategies, and apply sufficient effort and knowledge/skills to the team work. Because our factor analysis (previously described) included items related to different aspects of Hackman and Oldham's (1980) model on this factor, this enabling condition incorporated several concepts from the model (e.g., fostering commitment, inventing performance strategies, applying effort and knowledge/skills applied to the team's work, devising appropriate performance strategies, and working on meaningful tasks).

Therefore, it was conceptualized somewhat more broadly than in other studies (Hackman, 1990). Sample items from the 23-item scale are "The way we proceed with our work is fully appropriate for the tasks we have to do" and "Our current team enhances my professional commitment to education."

Enabling condition–contributing knowledge described the extent to which the team's work together enhanced the knowledge and skills of teachers and classified staff within the school and teaching and learning, as well as fostered shared knowledge and influence within the team. This variable was measured by six items. Sample items are "Our team has contributed to the knowledge and skills of teachers, classified staff" and "Our group has to deal with task problems for which we have not had sufficient training" (item reversed for coding).

Work Group Effectiveness (Dependent Variables)

Work group effectiveness was assessed by three variables: *performance effectiveness, team continuation,* and *team commitment.*

Performance effectiveness described the work produced by the team both in quality and quantity and was measured by the following two items: "We sometimes are told that our team does not produce enough work" (item reversed for coding) and "We sometimes are told that the quality of the work we produce is not satisfactory" (item reversed for coding).

Team continuation and team commitment dealt with members' desires to continue participating on the team and affective attachment to the team, and were measured by the following two items, respectively: "Given the way our team works together now, I would prefer not to continue to be a member of this team in the future" (item reversed for coding) and "I feel little commitment toward our work team" (item reversed for coding).

RESULTS

Intercorrelations, means, and standard deviations for the study variables are reported in Table 3.1. The *design features* were perceived on average to be moderately strong (means on six-point scales ranging from a low of 4.15 for group composition-size to a high of 5.03 for group composition-mix and task autonomy). Levels of *organizational support* and *task and interpersonal processes* were also in the moderate range (e.g., means ranging from a low of 4.03 for organizational support to a high of 4.79 for coordination of team/group norms). The three *enabling conditions'* means appeared moderately strong as well (e.g., 4.77 for contributing knowledge and 4.99 for team quality), as did mean scores for work group effectiveness (i.e., 4.95, 4.60, 4.53 for performance effectiveness, team continuation, and team commitment, respectively).

Means and standard deviations were also computed for individual items making up the study scales (see Table 3.2). Reliability coefficients using Cronbach's alpha coefficient for each scale are presented in Table 3.2. Several points appear notable with regard to the individual items.

First, with regard to items comprising *organizational support*, on the item asking whether the district went out of its way to show appreciation for good team performance, the mean was close to 3—"slightly disagree" (mean = 3.18). Somewhat higher was the perception that people who reviewed the team's work let the team know they liked what they did (mean = 4.15, close to "slightly agree"), nearly a one-point difference between means. Other means for items dealing with task requirements and training were close to 4.40, between "slightly agree" (4) and "agree" (5) on average, that the team received information about task expectations and training and technical consultation when needed. Thus, technical assistance and information about task requirements appeared more available, on average, than did rewards.

With regard to coordination of team/group norms, administrators rated perceptions of whether the team had clear standards for the behavior of team members near 5.0 on average, indicating "agreement." By contrast, coordination was somewhat more problematic, with respondents, on average, only between "slightly disagree" and "disagree" that coordination with other members was more trouble than it was worth (mean = 4.62, reversed scale), nearly a third of a point (.30) difference from the mean for clear standards.

With regard to the enabling condition-team quality, the lowest two means (4.60, 4.71) reflected general agreement that after an issue was raised, the team quickly reached a decision and that methods and procedures selected were appropriate for team tasks (between "slightly agree" and "agree"). By contrast, the highest means included perceptions that the team's work was meaningful and important and that members were willing to put in a "great deal of effort" to help the team fulfill its goals (5.34 and 5.48, between "agree" and "strongly agree"). Thus, there appeared to be less agreement about the appropriateness of particular methods than that individual members had the desire to help teams reach their objectives.

The patterns of correlations among design features, organizational support, task and interpersonal processes, enabling conditions, and work group effectiveness are also of interest in this study. Table 3.1 includes correlations among those variables that Hackman and Oldham's (1980) model conceptualized as antecedent to work group effectiveness.

Of 55 correlations among these (antecedent) study variables, 37 were statistically significant, indicating strong relationships among many of the model com-

Table 3.1. Descriptive Statistics and Intercorrelation Matrix for Study Variables (N = 76)

Variable	M	SD	1	2	3	4	5	6	7	8	9	10	11	12	13
1. Motivating Structure	5.01	1.21													
2. Group Composition-size	4.15	1.36	-.07												
3. Group Composition-mix	5.03	1.07	.37**	.14											
4. Task Autonomy	5.03	.76	.41**	.08	.41**										
5. Skill Complexity	4.93	1.38	.16	.17	.29*	.18									
6. Organizational Support	4.03	.94	.32**	.24*	.28*	.33**	.31**								
7. Coordination of Team	4.79	.91	.47**	.14	.44**	.33**	.08	.46**							
8. Knowledgeable Team	4.59	1.15	.34**	.09	.43**	.34**	.03	.44**	.45**						
9. Negative Conditions	2.41	1.11	-.22	.12	-.07	-.20	-.04	-.24*	-.30**	-.32**					
10. EC-team Quality	4.99	.67	.53**	.18	.46**	.55**	.28*	.49**	.55**	.60**	-.44**				
11. EC-contributing Knowledge	4.77	.73	.43**	.21	.35*	.55**	.22	.48**	.40**	.52**	-.33**	.73**			
12. Perf. Effectiveness	4.95	1.08	.10	.37**	.30**	.38**	.24*	.33**	.29*	.28*	-.07	.44**	.33**		
13. Team Commit.	4.53	1.02	.13	.04	.02	.31*	.20	.15	.16	.22	-.15	.33**	.33**	.24*	
14. Team Continuation	4.60	1.00	.32**	.12	.35**	.43**	-.01	.12	.42**	.42**	-.21	.59**	.45**	.35**	.36**

Note. *p<.05, **p< 01

Table 3.2 Descriptive Statistics of Items Used (N = 76)

Variables (1 = strongly disagree, 6 = strongly agree)	Mean	SD
Design Features		
Motivating Structure of Task		
1. We are a team of people with a shared task to perform—not a collection of individuals who have their own particular jobs to do.	5.01	1.21
Group Composition-Size *(Cronbach's alpha coefficient = .84)*		
1. Our admin. team is the right size to do our work well.	4.17	1.56
2. The size of our admin. team is (2 = too small, too large; 5 = about right)	4.13	1.37
Group Composition-Mix		
1. Our admin. team has the right mix of people needed to do our work well.	5.03	1.07
Task Autonomy *(Cronbach's alpha coefficient = .69)*		
1. Our team has the authority to manage our work pretty much the way we want to.	5.01	.87
2. There is a lot of room for initiative and judgment in the kind of work we do.	5.18	.81
3. Our admin. team merely carries out work; the principal decides what is to be done and how it is to be done (reverse).	4.88	1.18
Skill Complexity		
1. Members of our admin. team must use a number of complex and high-level skills to get our work done.	4.93	1.17
Organizational Support (Cronbach's alpha coefficient = .82)		
1. A team that does a good job in this organization does not get special rewards/recognition (reverse).	3.49	1.47
2. District goes out of its way to show appreciation for especially good performance by our admin. team.	3.18	1.35
3. People who receive/review team's work let us know they like what we do.	4.15	1.41
4. If our team does not know something it needs to know to do its work, there are people available to teach/help us.	4.46	1.12
5. It is often hard for our admin. team to figure out just what district management's real expectations and priorities are for our work (reverse).	4.45	1.20

Table 3.2 Descriptive Statistics of Items Used (N = 76)

Variables (1 = strongly disagree, 6 = strongly agree)	Mean	SD
6. If our team needs training/technical consultation to deal with a work-related problem, it is readily available to us.	4.42	1.20
Task and Interpersonal Processes Coordination of Team/ Group Norms *(Cronbach's alpha coefficient = .81)*		
1. It is difficult to communicate with other team members as much as I need to (reverse).	4.82	1.23
2. Our admin. team has clear standards for the behavior of admin. team members.	4.92	1.08
3. Sometimes coordinating with other members is more trouble than it's worth (reverse).	4.62	1.25
4. It is easy for our admin. team to tell if we are doing a good/bad job.	4.80	.97
Knowledgeable Team *(Cronbach's alpha coefficient = .59)*		
1. Some people in our admin. team do not have enough knowledge or skill to do their part of the group task (reverse).	4.87	1.24
2. People on our team share their special knowledge and expertise with each other.	4.32	1.56
Enabling Conditions		
Negative Conditions *(Cronbach's alpha coefficient = .71)*		
1. Our team could put substantially more effort into our work than we do at present.	2.14	1.16
2. Our team could bring more knowledge and skill to bear on the group task than we do at present.	2.67	1.36
Enabling Condition-Team Quality *(Cronbach's alpha coefficient = .96)*		
1. The team applies enough knowledge and skill to our work to get the task done well.	5.16	.85
2. Working with our team contributes to my own sense of personal well-being.	5.00	1.08
3. Our team has been very effective in accomplishing the goals it set for itself.	4.84	.92
4. Our team puts its plans into action in a timely manner.	4.90	.78
5. Team members work very hard to accomplish the tasks we are supposed to complete.	5.24	.83
6. Team members exhibit a great deal of skill in working on our group tasks.	4.89	.79

Table 3.2   Descriptive Statistics of Items Used (N = 76)

Variables (1 = strongly disagree, 6 = strongly agree)	Mean	SD
7. Working with our current team helps me learn new things that improve my job performance.	5.04	.94
8. I would like to keep working together with most of the members of the team.	5.27	.91
9. The way we proceed with our work is fully appropriate for the tasks we have to do.	4.99	.81
10. After an issue is raised, we quickly reach a decision as to what to do about it.	4.60	.97
11. Behavior in our admin. team is very orderly—it is clear what members are expected to do, and they do it.	5.07	.84
12. The work our admin. team does is meaningful and important.	5.34	.78
13. Our team's disciplinary strategies have promoted favorable student behavior in the school.	4.85	1.01
14. Our team works hard enough to get the task done well.	5.31	.75
15. The methods and procedures we use in working together are just right for the tasks we have to perform.	4.71	.76
16. Everyone in our work team cares about the group and works to make it one of the best.	5.04	1.03
17. Other team members value my input.	5.21	.74
18. I am willing to put in a great deal of effort to help our team fulfill its goals.	5.48	.65
19. Our current team enhances my professional commitment to education.	5.16	.92
20. When a nonroutine matter comes up in our work, we are quite adept at finding new ways to handle the situation.	5.00	.82
21. There is virtually no wasted effort in our group.	4.73	1.29
22. Team easily makes decisions about how to divide up tasks to accomplish the work.	4.75	1.03
23. There is a lot of jockeying for position in our admin. team (reverse).	5.24	1.13
Enabling Condition-Contributing Knowledge *(Cronbach's alpha coefficient = .83)*		
1. Our team's strategies have contributed to knowledge and skills of teachers.	4.97	.84
2. Our team has contributed to knowledge and skills of classified staff.	4.72	.89
3. Our team's strategies have promoted teaching and learning at the school.	4.95	1.00
4. There is a reasonable balance of influence among team members.	4.67	1.08

Table 3.2   Descriptive Statistics of Items Used (N = 76)

Variables (1 = strongly disagree, 6 = strongly agree)	Mean	SD
5. Our group has to deal with task problems for which we have not had sufficient training (reverse).	4.08	1.19
6. I am encouraged to share my knowledge in team meetings.	5.25	.98
Work Group Effectiveness		
Performance Effectiveness *(Cronbach's alpha coefficient = .86)*		
1. We sometimes are told that our team does not produce enough work (reverse).	4.04	1.12
2. We sometimes are told that the quality of the work we produce is not satisfactory (reverse).	3.85	1.19
Team Continuation		
1. Given the way our team works together now, I would prefer not to continue to be a member of the team in the future (reverse).	4.60	1.00
Team Commitment		
1. I feel little commitment toward our work team (reverse).	4.53	1.02

ponents (p < .05). The correlations among these model aspects ranged from a low of .03 (between skill complexity and knowledgeable team) to a high of .73 (between the two enabling conditions of team quality and contributing knowledge). Most correlations were in the moderate range, from .25 to .55 (p < .05).

Some of these patterns of correlations deserve mention, as they can contribute to analysis of construct validity (Glisson & Durick, 1988). The motivating structure of the task was unrelated to group size and skill complexity (r's = -.07 and .16) but was related to group composition-mix and task autonomy (r's = .37 and .41). This difference indicates no relationship between the extent to which an administrator perceives administrative tasks as a team effort (as opposed to an individual effort) and his or her view that group members are using complex skills —or the team is of appropriate size—but that those administrators who view members as a team also see their team as being able to take initiative and exercise judgment.

For example, in perceiving administration as a team effort, members may frequently consult each other about, for instance, student discipline violations, also providing a sense that the team can exercise initiative to resolve such problems.

It is also of interest to examine the correlations of the design features, organizational support, and task and interpersonal process variables with the *enabling conditions* (9 through 11 in Table 3.1). With regard to the negative conditions variable, organizational support, coordination of team/group norms, and knowledgeable team were significantly and inversely related to this variable (r's = -.24, -.30, and -.32, respectively) but not related to five others (motivational structure of the task, group composition [size, mix], task autonomy, and skill complexity).

This indicates that select "setup" features are important for influencing negative conditions; the perception that team members have expertise and special knowledge is inversely related, for example, to the feeling that more effort and knowledge/skill could be applied to team tasks. For the other two enabling conditions, all of the design features, organizational support, and task and interpersonal process variables (with the exceptions of group composition-size with team quality and group composition-size and skill complexity with contributing knowledge) are significantly correlated with team quality and contributing knowledge.

Finally, the correlates of the three *work group effectiveness* (dependent) variables were examined, utilizing both correlation and regression analyses to explore these relationships. For performance effectiveness, 9 of 11 correlations were statistically significant, with the strongest correlate being enabling condition-team quality with performance effectiveness (i.e., r = .44) (Table 3.1). Thus, those administrators who view their teams as applying sufficient effort, devising appropriate performance strategies, and fostering commitment also perceive the team as producing work of sufficient quantity and quality. However, the motivating structure of the task and the negative conditions were not significantly correlated with performance effectiveness.

For the team commitment variable, task autonomy and the enabling conditions of team quality and contributing knowledge were significantly correlated with team commitment (r's = .31, .33, and .33, respectively). However, the other study variables were not significantly associated with this variable.

For team continuation, seven variables had a significant correlation with this variable (r's = .32, .35, .43, .42, .42, .59, and .45), including motivating structure of the task, group composition-mix, task autonomy, coordination of team/group norms, knowledgeable team, enabling condition-team quality, and enabling condition-contributing knowledge. However, four variables (group composition-size, skill complexity, organizational support, and negative conditions) were not significantly correlated with team continuation. Interestingly, task autonomy had a significant correlation with both team commitment and team continuation, indicating that less discretion as a team is associated with lower feelings of commitment to, and desire to remain on, the team.

Finally, several multiple regression analyses were used to examine the predictive effects of model variables on our three work group effectiveness

Table 3.3   Regression Analysis: Variables Best Predicting Administrators' Perceptions of Performance Effectiveness (N = 76)

Variable	B	SE B	Beta	t value	p
Team size	.24	.08	.30	2.97	.004
Enabling condition-team quality	.44	.19	.27	2.27	.026

Note. R = .557; R^2 = .310; *Adj. R^2* = .281; *SE* = .918; *F ratio* = 10.643, *p* = .000.

Table 3.4   Regression Analysis: Variables Best Predicting Administrators' Perceptions of Team Continuation (N = 76)

Variable	B	SE B	Beta	t value	p
Enabling condition-team quality	.61	.210	.40	2.88	.005

Note. R = .617; R^2 = .381; *Adj. R^2* = .346; *SE* = .809; *F ratio* = 10.773, *p* = .000.

dimensions.[3] Final models incorporating previously significant predictors for each work group effectiveness dimension are discussed here. For performance effectiveness, *group composition-size* and *enabling condition-team quality* emerged as significant positive predictors of performance effectiveness in the presence of other variables in the equation (ß = .30, p < .01; ß = .27, p < .05) (see Table 3.3).

Further, for team continuation, *enabling condition-team quality* emerged as a significant positive predictor of team continuation in the final model (ß = .40, p < .01) (Table 3.4). These final regression models predicted a fairly sizable portion (28% and 35%, adjusted R^2, respectively) of the variance in performance effectiveness and team continuation. For team commitment, when the previously significant correlates were combined in a regression model, none of the variables emerged as significant.

The final models suggest that the team characteristics that are most critical for performance effectiveness are different from those for desire to remain on the team (team continuation). Although the *enabling condition-team quality* is a predictor of both outcomes, performance effectiveness is also influenced by *team size*, a design feature. Perhaps because this outcome deals with the quantity (amount) and quality of work, given high administrative workloads, the appropriate group size becomes critical.

For team continuation, by contrast, a feeling on the part of the administrator that, given the way the team works together, he/she would prefer (or not prefer) to continue membership, the *quality* of the team's working efforts— ability to work together to apply effort and strategies, to foster commitment, and to work on meaningful tasks—becomes most critical.

CONCLUSION AND IMPLICATIONS

We began this chapter by stating that current and projected shortages of administrators in our nation's schools are prompting renewed thinking about the design of these administrative jobs. This chapter suggests that one aspect of administrative work design is the creation and nurturing of high-functioning teams. Administrative teams that engage their members seem likely to increase member effectiveness as well as to create an atmosphere conducive to career leadership positions.

Conversely, ineffective teams appear costly to school systems. They tend to disenfranchise new and seasoned administrators, leading to their early career departure, necessitating a renewed and costly search for, and socialization of, their replacements. "Stressful" administrator jobs that are demanding in terms of time and energy suggest that high salary levels will not be enough to entice prospective administrators into the positions and encourage them to remain (ERS, 2000, p. 26).

A limitation to this study was the relatively small sample for the factor analysis, a procedure that typically requires over 150 respondents. Future research using larger sample sizes with ample data should be carried out to validate or replicate these research findings. Further, team perceptions according to age, gender, and work experience of administrators (Leach & Cooper, 2011) and the mediating effect of enabling conditions (Hackman & Oldham, 1980) should be examined.

A central study finding was that site administrators had generally positive perceptions of the teams they were on. For example, survey responses were close to "agree" (5) on average that administrators seemed a "team of people" with a shared task, that teams had the correct "mix" of people to do administrative work, and that teams possessed the authority to manage the work and develop work procedures. In terms of how teams worked together, administrators also had positive perceptions about communication ("disagreeing" on average that they encountered problems communicating with others as needed).

Teams were also perceived to have clear standards for behavior. However, "coordinating with other members" was somewhat more problematic, with administrators only indicating between on average "slightly disagree" and "disagree" that coordination was sometimes more trouble than it was worth.

The study has implications for creating strategies that districts and/or sites might use to build administrative teams. First, *enhanced attention should be directed to how administrative teams are rewarded and recognized for their efforts.* On average, administrators "slightly disagreed" that districts went out of their way to show appreciation for good team performance (3.18). Districts that accord rewards and recognition, for example, to principals but not the team, might only encourage individuals to "differentiate themselves from the team effort" (Hackman, 1990, p. 11).

Further, the strengthening of team efforts by allocating rewards and recognition might be important to both novice and veteran administrators. Novices are likely interested in seeking assurances that the work they are doing is considered valuable and worthwhile, and veteran administrators may have worked hard at inducting and fully including novice administrators on their teams (Pellicer & Nemeth, 1980).

Second, *districts should remain open to team recommendations for altering working conditions to meet team responsibilities.* With regard to organizational support items about task requirements and assistance—and using training/technical consultation when needed—mean scores were only slightly higher than rewards and recognition, between "slightly agree" and "agree" (e.g., between 4.42 and 4.46).

Considering the changing demands—when "new expectations" are often added onto traditional ones with little "consideration of whether the new role in its entirety is feasible under the current working conditions faced"—administrative work teams require information from districts about task requirements and constraints as well as training and technical assistance (Fullan, 2007, p. 168). As Fullan notes, by remaining open to teams' recommendations for altering the working conditions to meet their responsibilities, districts could focus on providing assistance "at the group's initiative," as opposed to district administration determining when the administrative team should receive it (Hackman, 1990, p. 11).

Third, *design efforts should focus on the contribution and development of knowledge both within and outside the team.* Collinson and Cook (2007) observed that one of the fastest ways for an organization to "lose high-performing principals and teachers . . . can occur when school conditions do not allow them to grow and, by extension, prevent them from helping students and colleagues to learn" (p. 188). Our contributing knowledge variable assessed perceptions that the team had enhanced the knowledge and skills of not only administrators but also teachers and support personnel and had strengthened teaching and learning in the school.

Our study findings suggest that effective work teams work well together and demonstrate commitment to their joint efforts (team quality), but they also progress beyond the boundaries of their team to further the growth of others in the school organization.

Fourth, *attempts should be made to avoid self-reinforcing downward performance spirals on administrative teams* (Hackman, 1990). These spirals are evidenced by team members' perceptions that other members are not fully bringing their effort and knowledge and skills to bear on team tasks (negative conditions). In this study, three variables were correlates of these conditions: lack of organizational support, lack of coordination of team/group norms, and insufficient team knowledge.

Remedies for coordination might include, for example, the deployment of support staff in scheduling and other supports and group meetings devoted to coordination of the team's work. These measures might bring to a halt negative spirals—that is, "process losses that waste effort"—and renew commitment to the group and its task: "a process gain that can build effort" (Hackman, 1990, p. 12).

Finally, *effective group design should not only be directed toward efficiency of group or individual efforts but also toward human satisfaction and adjustment to the work.* Some time ago, Porter, Lawler, and Hackman (1975) observed that "routine, repetitive, and simplified" work design, for example, would be likely to reduce personal satisfaction on the job, thereby creating organizational costs (p. 284). They maintained that efficiency and satisfaction must be combined: "neither a grossly inefficient job which makes employees joyously happy nor a highly efficient job which is dissatisfying and frustrating to employees is likely to be facilitative of long-term organizational effectiveness" (Porter et al., 1976, p. 284).

In this study, perceptions that teams directed their own work and exercised initiative and judgment (task autonomy) were associated with administrators' views that sufficient progress was being made toward team goals (efficiency) and that they were committed to and desirous of staying on their teams (satisfaction) (Table 3.1). However, team size was related to the effectiveness dimension but not the commitment dimension of satisfaction. Primary consideration might be given to those design features that maximize a combination of these outcomes.

To summarize, administrative teams fit the definition of work teams in organizations, as they are intact social systems, have members with differentiated roles, and exercise collective responsibility for the leadership and administration of the school. Teams appear to play a key role in an administrator's work experience, but insufficient attention has been accorded to them. Greater emphasis might be placed by district officials and site team members on being responsive (Conley & Cooper, this volume) to the needs of administrators working in teams.

As one administrator responding to our survey described the effect of her administrative work team in a written comment: "I am fortunate to be a member of an exceptionally cohesive team. I would leave this team only in the event of a promotion. We team members *like* each other, *support* each other, and *complement* each other's strengths." We hope this chapter has taken a step toward assisting schools to realize this promise.

REFERENCES

Association of California School Administrators. (2008). *New program encourages principal leadership*. Retrieved February 24, 2010 from www.acsa.org/FunctionalMenu-Categories/Media/EdCalNewspaper/2008/Oct27/Principalprogram.aspx.

Babbie, E. R. (1973). *Survey research methods*. Belmont, CA: Wadsworth Publishing Co.

Bauer, S. C., & Bogotch, I. (2001). Analysis of the relationships among site council resources, council practices, and outcomes. *Journal of School Leadership 11*, 98–119.

Beehr, T. A. (1995). *Psychological stress in the workplace*. London: Routledge.

Bolman, L. G., & Deal, T. E. (2003). *Reframing organizations: Artistry, choice, and leadership*. San Francisco: Jossey-Bass.

Campbell, L. (2001). The best leaders: Learning from the best. *Association of California School Administrators, 37*(3), 7.

Christensen, M. M. (2002). *Effective comprehensive high school administration teams*. Unpublished doctoral dissertation, University of California, Santa Barbara.

Collinson, V., Cook, T. F. (2007). *Organizational learning: Improving learning, teaching, and leading in school systems*. Thousand Oaks, CA: Sage.

Conley, S., Fauske, J., & Pounder, D. G. (2004). Teacher work group effectiveness. *Educational Administration Quarterly, 40*(5), 663–703.

Conley, S., Shaw, S., & Glasman, N. (2007). Correlates of job and growth satisfaction among a sample of secondary school administrators. *Journal of School Leadership 17*(1), 54–88.

Cooley, V. E., & Shen, J. (2003). School accountability and professional job responsibilities: A perspective from secondary principals. *NASSP Bulletin, 87*(634), 10–25.

Crow, H. M., & Pounder, D. G. (2000). Interdisciplinary teacher teams: Context, design, and process. *Educational Administration Quarterly 36*, 216–254.

Eckman, E. W. (2004). Similarities and differences in role conflict, role commitment, and job satisfaction for female and male high school principals. *Educational Administration Quarterly 40*(3), 366–387.

Educational Research Service. (2000). *The principal, keystone of a high-achieving school: Attracting and keeping the leaders we need*. Arlington, VA: Educational Research Service, National Association of Elementary School Principals, and National Association of Secondary School Principals.

Fullan, M. (2007). *The new meaning of educational change, 4th edition*. New York: Teachers College Press.

Glisson, C., & Durick, M. (1988). Predictors of job satisfaction and organizational commitment in human service organizations. *Administrative Sciences Quarterly, 33*(1), 61–81.

Grubb, W. N., & Flessa, J. (2006). "A job too big for one": Multiple principals and other nontraditional approaches. *Educational Administration Quarterly, 42*, 518–550.

Hackman, J. R. (1982). *A set of methods for research on work teams*. New Haven, CT: Technical Report No. 1, Group Effectiveness Project, School of Organization and Management, Yale University.

Hackman, J. R. (1990). *Groups that work (and those that don't)*. San Francisco: Jossey-Bass.

Hackman, J. R., & Oldham, G. R. (1980). *Work redesign*. Reading, MA: Addison-Wesley.

Hulin, C. L., Roznowski, M., & Hachiya, D. (1985). Alternative opportunities and withdrawal decisions: Empirical and theoretical discrepancies and an integration. *Psychological Bulletin, 97*(2), 233–250.

Leach, D., & Cooper, B. S. (2011). Assistant superintendents moving to the superintendency. In S. Conley & B. S. Cooper (Eds.), *Finding, Preparing, and Supporting School Leaders*. Lanham, MD: Rowman & Littlefield.

Pellicer, L. O., & Nemeth, G. (1980). Tired of carrying the world on your shoulders? Try team management. *NASSP Bulletin, 64*(439), 97–102.

Porter, L. W., Lawler, E. E., & Hackman, J. R. (1975). *Behavior in organizations*. New York: McGraw Hill.

Pounder, D. G. (1999). Teacher teams: Exploring job characteristics and work-related outcomes of work group enhancement. *Educational Administration Quarterly, 35*(3), 317–348.

Pounder, D. G., & Merrill, R. J. (2001). Job desirability of the high school principalship: A job choice theory perspective. *Educational Administration Quarterly, 37*(1), 27–57.

Spillane, J. (2001). Investigating school leadership practice: A distributed perspective. *Educational Researcher, 30*(3), 23–28.

Vinokur-Kaplan, D. (1995). Treatment teams that work (and those that don't): An application of Hackman's group effectiveness model to interdisciplinary teams in psychiatric hospitals. *Journal of Applied Behavioral Science, 31*, 303–327.

Chapter Four

Leading in Financially Stressful Times

Rick Ginsberg and Karen D. Multon

There's a tidal wave coming. And it's about to affect *your* kids. In recent weeks, state education funding woes have triggered a tsunami of pink slips to thousands upon thousands of teachers and support staff in school districts statewide, with about 9,800 layoffs of teachers so far. Another 1,600 retiring teachers won't be replaced. Total planned layoffs stand at more than 17,000 school personnel. And that's just with 75 percent of districts responding to a survey sent by a coalition of education groups. When all is said and done, school layoffs statewide could top 20,000, the coalition warns.

—Maudlyne Ihejirika, *Chicago Sun-Times*, March 28, 2010,
article on effects of budget cuts on Illinois' schools

The U.S. economy has struggled over the past two years, facing a Wall Street meltdown, housing slump, bailouts of major corporations, mortgage defaults, high unemployment rates, and weakened consumer confidence. The result has been a significant decline in tax receipts for many states, which impacts funding for both P–12 schools and higher education. According to the Rockefeller Institute's State Revenue Flash Report for the fourth quarter of 2009, state tax revenues declined in 39 of 46 reporting states (February 23, 2010—retrieved at www.rockinst.org).

The same report indicated that year-to-year employment growth for the nation declined almost continuously from the first quarter of 2006 through the fourth quarter of 2009. Two-thirds of those school districts responding to an American Association of School Administrators (AASA) survey indicated having to eliminate positions for the 2009–2010 school year, with the percentage of districts reducing staff levels, furloughing personnel, and laying off personnel increasing during the past year (Ellerson & McCord, 2009).

Education Week reported that about half the states are poised to slash spending on K–12 in fiscal 2011 (Maxwell, March 1, 2010).

In higher education, where state support for public colleges and universities has been on a steady decline for years, state economic woes have resulted in cuts at the same time that the demands for a more educated workforce are increasing (Clark, 2009). The Center on Budget Policy and Priorities (Johnson, Oliff, & Williams, 2010) recently reported that more states (39) cut higher education spending than other services (K–12—29 states, health care—29 states, and services to the elderly and disabled—24 states).

California, for example, along with limiting enrollment in certain of its colleges and universities, raised tuition at the University of California institutions by a whopping 32 percent. And with stimulus funds that have supported many state budgets expiring next year, the situation may worsen even if the economy begins to turn around.

Working in such an atmosphere of decline can't be fun. With the constant barrage of news information about federal and state budget woes and potential cuts and layoffs, maintaining morale in most any organization has to be a challenge, adding a whole new layer of concerns for leaders hoping to maintain productivity with fewer resources. This situation is especially problematic for administrators of public P–12 and higher education institutions due to the severity of state budget cutbacks in many regions of the country in the face of increasing demands for accountability.

Two main strands of research over the past 30 years provide leaders with some insights related to dealing with difficult economic conditions. The first is the research on *cutback leadership or management*, which was popularized during the 1980s in a prior recession (Levine, 1978; Levine, 1979; McTighe, 1979; Biller, 1980; Bombyk & Chernesky, 1985). More recently, in related tones, popular media articles on managing decline have emerged (Leaman, 2008; Hopkins, 2008; Charan & Colvin, 2001; Richman & Davis, 1995). These studies provide a series of strategies for dealing with budget cutbacks and maintaining staff morale in the face of decline.

The second area is what has been labeled as *crisis management*, mostly focusing on leadership in response to large-scale tragedies like the terrorist attacks of 9/11, mad cow disease, hurricanes and tsunamis, the Chernobyl disaster, and other high-profile crises that shocked nations (Smith & Elliott, 2006; Coombs, 1999; Robert & Lajtha, 2002; Stern & Sundelius, 2002). But within the research are ideas for dealing with crises analogous to the economic turmoil facing educational institutions today.

All these lines of research focus a good deal of attention on maintaining staff morale (Behn, 1980; Sullivan, 2008). Whether the crisis be economic, social, political, or involve loss of life or property, it is emphasized that leaders must find ways to keep organizations on track despite the difficult times. Interestingly, however, little attention is paid to the impact on leaders who are having to guide an organization through economic difficulties. Surely, if staff morale is depicted as important, it is appropriate to assume that leader morale is similarly significant. Leaders are clearly vital to the success of an organization, and their centrality is likely more important during a fiscal or other crisis. Only recently has any research examined the impact on leaders of making difficult decisions (Ginsberg & Davies, 2007) or the emotional skills needed for working with employees (Caruso & Salovey, 2004; Goleman, Boyatzis, & McKee, 2002), but even this research did not specifically examine the difficulty for leadership during tough budget times.

The focus of the research in this chapter is on one portion of a study examining how leaders of K–12 and higher education institutions are dealing with their roles and responsibilities during a difficult financial period. The research examined the perspectives of samples of principals, superintendents, university department chairs, and deans of schools/colleges of education. Several questions guided the research:

1. What has been the degree of budget cuts that the program has experienced?
2. How have leaders dealt with meeting the cuts imposed?
3. How have the cuts affected the organization?
4. How have the cuts affected leaders?

The data reported in this chapter focus on the responses from the principals, including principals from the Minneapolis–St. Paul metropolitan area who responded to a survey of 95 items including both forced-choice and open-ended questions. The forced-choice questions included those collecting demographic information, data about job satisfaction and general health, perceptions of the impact of cuts, and several questions from surveys with validated measures of work-related flow, general affective disposition, and perceived ability to overcome obstacles to goals. In addition, several open-ended questions sought more details about the degree of budget cuts, what actions were taken, and the impact of these cuts on leaders and their organizations.

Follow-up telephone interviews were conducted with a small sample of those willing to participate. A total of about 300 principals (included were some other school leaders) were contacted via e-mail to respond to the web-based survey. Of these, we included 93 principals in our analysis, representing a 31% response rate, though the actual response rate of principals is a bit higher, as many on the e-mail list were not serving in principal roles and we did not include their responses in our analysis.

RESEARCH RELATED TO DEALING WITH BUDGET CUTS

Many popular magazines today offer tips for leaders on how to deal with the financial crisis facing education and most every field. These sources agree that today's leaders are ill equipped for handling the economic situations they face. Leaman (2008), for example, suggested that most managers don't know how to handle a recession. He wrote, "A survey by consultancy Pentacle earlier this year suggested that as many as 70% of managers do not know how to react" (p. 14).

The research most closely aligned with an understanding of how leaders today might deal with budget cuts is derived from earlier studies on what was labeled as cutback leadership/management, and later, crisis management. The cutback leadership/management literature evolved during an earlier economic downturn in the late 1970s. Levine (1979) popularized the term "cutback management" in a call for research on what he described as fiscally stressed public organizations.

He argued that cutback management means "managing organizational change toward lowered levels of resource consumption and organizational activity" (p. 180). According to Behn (1980), the real challenge for leaders is to help turn the organization "into one that is smaller, doing less, consuming fewer resources, but still doing something and doing it well" (p. 614). Most of the literature identified a lack of direction for leaders in dealing with the economic crisis. McTighe (1979) lamented the lack of formal training for leaders in managing under conditions of declining rather than growing resources. Several researchers identified the ill effects on workers and their morale during difficult economic times (Bombyk & Chernesky, 1985; McTighe, 1979).

Crisis management is a newer field that focuses on easing the potential impact of various kinds of crises or disasters. Most of the literature suggests that no more than 50% of companies have crisis management plans in place (Kash & Darling, 1998; Preble, 1997). According to Coombs (1999), crisis management represents a set of factors designed to minimize the effects of a crisis. He argued, "crisis management seeks to prevent or lessen the negative outcomes of a crisis and thereby protect the organization, stakeholders, and/or industry from damage" (p. 4). He suggested four basic factors in crisis management—prevention, preparation, performance, and learning.

Based on research on industrial crises, Miller (2006) found three types of crises—financial, psychological or interpersonal, and societal and environmental. Smith (2006) identified three distinct phases within the crisis management process—a precrisis phase (which includes warning of a pending crisis), a period of crisis impact or rescue, and lastly a period of crisis management with a view toward recovery or demise.

Preble's (1997) review of relevant literature discovered several elements of crisis management: the crisis audit, crisis management team, management plans, crisis readiness, disaster recovery, activities of crisis preparedness, and crisis protocols. He suggested a very linear process similar to contingency planning in the financial sector, which included contingency planning, risk assessment, developing alternative strategies, planning documentation, and testing. Others have offered similar types of approaches for dealing with crises that organizations face (Hickman & Crandall, 1997; Kash & Darling, 1998; Robert & Lajtha, 2002; Sapriel, 2003).

What none of the literature addresses, however, is how leaders themselves are affected by leading in times of cutbacks or other crises. Several studies emphasized the need to bolster worker morale, but none highlighted the impact and dangers for those who must lead their organizations through fiscal crises or other disasters. This research examines one form of crisis—financial—and how leaders in education settings deal with and are impacted during such upheaval.

FINDINGS: THE NEW NORMAL

The principals who responded were 57% female, had served as a principal for an average of 11.42 years and 7.27 years in their current role. The average budget cuts they had faced were 5.32% last year, an additional 7.51% during the current year. Thus, without knowing what next year's budget might be, the principals indicated that, on average, they had experienced 12.83% budget cuts over the past two years.

Concerning job satisfaction, Table 4.1 reports the results of the data the principals provided. As noted, principals reported relatively strong levels of enjoyment of their position and satisfaction with their performance. However, the results suggest low levels of satisfaction with personal time (defined as leisure, relaxation, and other aspects of their personal lives). Of course, such results are difficult to interpret without baseline data from prior to the current

Table 4.1   Principal Satisfaction (scale: 1 = very low to 7 = very high)

	Mean
Enjoyment with position	6.33 (SD = .91)
Satisfaction with performance	5.77 (SD = 1.07)
Satisfaction with personal time	3.19 (SD = 1.86)

period of budget declines, but the results do display a clear sense that principals like their work, feel good about what they do, but wish they had more time for themselves.

We posed several questions for the principals on the impact of budget cuts on their physical health. The results were somewhat mixed on these questions. Regarding their feelings about their physical health, the principals indicated that they were between average and somewhat better than average (3.65 on a scale of 1 = Poor to 5 = Much Better Than Average). However, on a question about how their health has been affected by budget cuts, the principals indicated that their health had gotten a little worse due to budget cuts (2.46 on a scale of 1 = much worse to 5 = much better). Indeed, 56% of the principals indicated that their health had gotten worse due to budget cuts. And when asked if they worry about their health, the principals indicated they do (5.20 on a scale of 1 [definitely false] to 8 [definitely true]).

Table 4.2 reports the results to questions on the impact of budget cuts. The results here are mixed as well. Clearly, the principals are most concerned about the challenges they face as a result of the budget cuts (5.28 on the 1 to 7 scale). Issues such as efforts to implement innovations (4.93), services being offered (4.89), and faculty and staff morale (4.44) were most affected by the cuts. On the other hand, conflict levels (3.97), personal job satisfaction (3.93), relations with employees (3.76), and employee-to-employee relations (3.46) are reportedly less affected as a result of the cuts the principals have experienced.

Table 4.2   Impact of Budget Cuts on Principals (scale: 1 = no impact, 7 = very high)

Ranked by Mean	Mean
Challenges faced as a leader	5.28 (SD = 1.39)
Efforts to implement innovations	4.93 (SD = 1.66)
Services offered by your institution	4.89 (SD = 1.56)
Morale of faculty and staff	4.44 (SD = 1.62)
Your organizational mission	4.35 (SD = 1.58)
Your morale	4.23 (SD = 1.50)
Employee job satisfaction	4.20 (SD = 1.49)
Organizational strategic planning	4.14 (SD = 1.60)
Employee enjoyment of work	4.11 (SD = 1.37)
Your enjoyment of work	4.06 (SD = 1.50)
Conflict levels in your organizational setting	3.97 (SD = 1.62)
Your job satisfaction	3.93 (SD = 1.50)
Your relations with employees	3.76 (SD = 1.72)
Employee to employee relations	3.46 (SD = 1.37)

While the ongoing nature of the financial problems facing states will likely continue for the foreseeable future, these data suggest a mixed impact of budget cuts to this point. The principals appear to enjoy their jobs (on another scale they reported getting a great deal of motivation from their work), they are satisfied with their performance (another scale indicated that the principals feel they are able to solve problems), and workplace relations seem not to have broken down even in the current climate. These are what we consider positive outcomes that were reported.

On the other hand, a number of disturbing results emerged as well. The principals reported serious concerns about time for leisure, relaxation, and personal life. They implied that their physical health had been affected. And finally, they reported significant challenges in areas like making innovative reforms, services offered, and overall faculty and staff morale. These findings are the type that will likely result in negative consequences for students and classrooms.

To explore these findings in greater detail, especially those we labeled as the disturbing results, the open-ended questions provided opportunities for the principals to provide more information about how budget cuts were impacting their work lives. The overarching theme we derived we call *trying to find the new normal*. Principal after principal described a situation that was in flux, that had no clear ending in sight, and that was creating increasing levels of concern for them and the faculty and staff they served. For example, one principal described the sentiment in this manner:

> It is very hard to keep the herd moving in the same direction with less and less support and with the prospect of tougher working conditions in a time when our accountability and scrutiny is at an all-time high. Morale is low in the area of hope for the future. I cannot stress the fact enough our staff gives their all . . . but I think we are all feeling like we are rearranging deck chairs on the Titanic. We feel like our ship is sinking, but we are going to do all that we can until it does.

Another principal presented the situation in equally stark terms:

> I had to make hard decisions to balance the budget. I worked to make the cuts affect the office and support staff and kept the regular classroom untouched . . . the impact was that people felt there was lessened support to classroom teachers. The conflict is a form of grieving loss and frustration in doing more with less time and resources. The conflict feels as though staff are fighting to have back what was—that's human nature. I have tried to lessen the impact on them and have taken on more myself by finding grant support, reconfiguring positions, always thinking about what else could support the school. The impact of the stress is with me all the time.

We characterize the theme of *trying to find the new normal* as having four components. First, there was a consistent sense reported from a majority of principals that everyone is working hard to do more with less. Second, the principals were clear that despite the assertions to the contrary, all cuts affect students and teachers. Third, the principals described intense levels of anger, often directed at them. We call this "tornadoes of negativity." And finally, the principals reported a growing concern with the levels of stress for both them and their faculty and staff. We explore each of these components next.

The principals shared a pervasive concern about having to continue to work hard or harder with fewer and fewer resources. For many, the real concern was meeting the No Child Left Behind (NCLB) demand for accountability (most notably Annual Yearly Progress [AYP]) while the very resources that were put in place to help with these matters were among the first things eliminated. It seemed almost cruel in its effects. Several comments that the principals shared with us will illustrate this component of the new normal:

- "We are expected to do more and more with less and less, and the challenges are not getting any less while societal pressures on staff and students increase."
- "It is difficult to afford what we need to meet the students' needs."
- "Everyone is exhausted and working harder than ever with less."
- "NCLB nails us with AYP—yet we can't provide programming to overcome the challenges."
- "Everyone has to work more to accomplish with less time and money. This causes employees stress. Future budget cuts will lead to job cuts . . . and more stress."
- "Teachers have to deal with AYP issues after they have lost significant programs that provided interventions. We are faced with having to do more with less resources, yet we are also expected to NEVER use lack of resources as an excuse for not making AYP."
- "Increased class sizes create more climate issues and reduce the ability of staff to meet the needs of students. This impacts staff as well as administration, due to the need to pick up the pieces to ensure that staff can focus on instruction rather than behavior consequences. Staff are more stressed, busier, have less time to interact on a social level, and demonstrate less job satisfaction and lower morale . . ."

Second, despite a great deal of rhetoric to the contrary, while political leaders always talk about making cuts that do not impact students and classrooms, the principals were adamant that all cuts, no matter where they are made, have an effect on students and teachers. Those who make such statements about cuts not hurting classrooms were described as not really understanding schools. Note these comments by several of the principals:

- "All services impact teachers and students. That is what we are really learning this year. It is impossible to make cuts in a district and not have it impact teachers and students. We cut a secretary, and many tasks are now falling to teachers. This takes up their precious time to prepare for students. We cut a technology integration person, and now teachers are having to spend more time researching websites and online projects. We cut a mail delivery person, and now secretaries and [paraprofessionals] are having to do curbside pickup and drop-off of mail so the mail can travel on buses. It has further added to our already reduced office staff."
- "We transferred interventions from the intervention specialists to the classroom teachers; reduction of materials has led to less communication with parents; larger classes have results—36 in fifth grade!"
- "Increased class sizes, reduction in support services, more students working with support staff during intervention time, less opportunities for 'bubble kids' who need extra help to meet grade level benchmarks."
- "I chose licensed staff over paraprofessional support with interventions. The specialist class was not in a room as it has been in previous years and results in a less desirable learning space."

Third, we discovered that a number of principals were very optimistic about how well their respective staffs had pulled together in the face of enormous economic pressure to move forward. One typical comment along these lines highlighted "how staff rally together to get the work done." But a far larger percentage of principals were concerned about the negativity that the cuts were generating. These principals were very stressed by the reactions their colleagues, faculty, and support staff (Conley, Gould, & Levine, 2010) were having to the reductions. One described it this way: "Tornadoes of negativity are hard to be around. There are reduced levels of trust with employees." Others were similarly stressed:

- "I felt attacked by teachers who believed I played a role in decisions."
- "I was on the budget team and I felt like other administrators who weren't on the team acted like I made the choices—or pitched a vote—to cut items and not cut others. That was certainly not the case."
- "A large part of my job is working with people so that various viewpoints are heard. I also spend a lot of time keeping peace among various employees."
- "I was and continue to be surprised at how some people react. I had typically reasonable people telling me that they weren't going to do their

job—because it wasn't fair for a program or person to be cut. It has been hard to rally the troops around a positive mission . . . I feel we have taken a huge step backwards in our communication, trust, and cooperation. So we have more work to do and are working together more poorly."

Finally, the principals described a situation where stress levels were on the rise. For example, a total of 70% of participants used the word *stress* (54%) or described stress-related symptoms (16%) in answering the question on how their physical health was impacted by budget cuts. Another 16% of participants lamented the lack of time for exercise. Principals indicated they felt tired most the time (5.35 on a 1 to 8 scale), and that they usually found themselves worrying about something (5.5 on 1 to 8 scale). The comments they shared were especially troubling in terms of the stress levels that were brewing:

- "I don't sleep at night. I get little exercise. I don't take vacations because I think I shouldn't. I don't spend quality time with my family."
- "The stress of the job has affected my blood pressure even more than it was."
- "I don't have time to exercise or even eat lunch most days. I have gained five pounds that on a small frame is not good."
- "Although my physical health has significantly deteriorated, my mental health is affected greatly during stressful times such as budget cuts and impacts my physical health as I don't eat well and am not inclined to exercise."
- "Because of the long hours at work, I have to choose between exercise or sleep. . . . I choose sleep."
- "More stress has caused headaches, backaches, anxiety, and sleeplessness."
- "Less excitement for work. Not exercising as much as I used to."

Taken together, what we describe as the "new normal" suggests that principals facing a prolonged period of tight or shrinking budgets are scurrying to cope with a reality far different from anything they have faced before. They clearly are having to perform the same tasks, in some cases more tasks and responsibilities, with fewer resources. They realize that despite comments about cuts not impacting students, all cuts impact classrooms, teachers, and students. Sadly, many are facing waves of negativity over things that weren't their initiative, and the result appears to be increased levels of tension and stress in the workplace.

HARBINGERS OF HOPE—COPING DURING THE STORM

What struck us in analyzing these data was the resiliency of so many of the principals. Despite all the negativity and the anxiety that accompanies a new set of circumstances, many were successfully coping with the situation. The Minneapolis–St. Paul metropolitan area principals offered three main approaches for successfully dealing with the tough budget times: adopt a "can-do" attitude, plan and offer transparency in ongoing communications, and make certain to take care of yourself. The can-do attitude was especially encouraging. The principals strongly indicated (on a 1 to 8 scale) that:

- "Even when others get discouraged, I know I can find a way to solve the problem" (6.41).
- "I can think of many ways to get out of a jam" (6.76).
- "I energetically pursue my goals" (6.76).

In describing the situation, their responses displayed an optimistic approach to the situation at hand, with a supportive and encouraging attitude. Here is a sample of those comments:

- "Push forward with a positive attitude to keep things going well for students."
- "Sometimes you really can do more with less. You just have to get through the whining and the 'I can't do its' that accompany change."
- "I try to support the teachers in their added roles and demonstrate that I am also taking on extra duties."
- "Talk as much as I can without making it seem like the sky is falling. I want staff to feel continued support . . ."
- "The most critical thing we can do is to support our staff and find ways to be encouraging."
- "I approach the cuts with a 'can-do' attitude to keep everyone's hope alive and put a positive spin on the challenge, reassuring the staff . . ."

The notion of being certain to carefully plan and display real transparency in all communications was a second coping strategy the principals employed. In terms of planning, they were pretty consistent about the need for being open and utilizing some forward thinking. Note these samples of remarks by the principals: "A key is planning for the worst case scenario"; "I met with the building level team, including parent representatives, to brainstorm and make recommendations for budget cuts"; "Have open discussion, make no promises except to try hard to make the process and the cuts as painless as possible. Allowing voice is the most important part of the process."

Related to this, the principals emphasized the need for complete transparency in discussing issues with faculty and staff and other constituents. This strategy not only allowed them to gather more information, it made everyone a part of the process. Note these remarks:

- "Communication and gathering input is extremely important, and you can't do it enough. I also think that being transparent is the key."
- "Communicate, communicate!! I let them know what is happening and squash rumors that may abound . . ."
- "Don't be afraid to talk openly early in the process. It will cause turmoil, but in the end the reaction is more accepted."
- "Difficult decisions can be made if communication is open."
- "I used the site council as a sounding board. Tried to be transparent throughout the entire process."

A third coping strategy was clear. Nearly all the principals talked about the need to take care of themselves. Several discussed the notion of being certain to maintain balance in life, while others just highlighted ideas and approaches that worked for them. In terms of balance in life, they indicated:

- "I need to keep balance—life is bigger than this position . . . even though I implemented decisions, I didn't get much support along the way."
- "Taking a breath often and thinking of all the good that we offer kids on a daily basis. Walk and interact with the kids every day. They provide the hope, the reason we do this. I recognize it could be worse and do the best with what we have."
- "Manage what I can, accept what I can't control, and make the best of the situation. Know that I am doing the best to set the priorities where they need to be . . ."
- "I make sure to spend time outside each day getting fresh air. I continue to greet the students each morning as they arrive. I maintain a balance between my hours at work and my house away from work."
- "Immerse myself in my family when time allows. I put in on average 65 hours a week on the job. I have learned that when I go home, I leave work out of my family time."
- "A loving family and dog! The more you do this job, the more you need balance, confidence, and the ability to think creatively."

Their means for taking care of themselves were fairly consistent and mostly involved making time to talk to others and exercise. The sense was that leaders didn't have to go through the difficult time alone, and relying on friends and colleagues was a viable means for dealing with the tension. And exercise, a proven stress reducer, was mentioned by a large number of the principals. Here are a few samples of their comments about taking care of yourself: "Checking in with mentors"; "Connect with principal colleagues"; Talking to colleagues and spouse"; "Exercise"; "Communicate with people around you and listen without defense"; "Daily and weekly routines of quiet time, exercise, and family time. Focus on the positive. I write thank you notes to staff every week and try to recognize success we are achieving in our school in spite of the cuts. I have strong friendship ties that I maintain with other women leaders. They are a great sounding board, sharing their own struggles so I don't feel isolated"; "Leave work at home. Make myself go home. Exercise"; "Much discussion with other elementary principals in the district, including looking to them for support."

CONCLUSION

The purpose of the study reported in this chapter was to examine how going through difficult budget cuts is affecting the principals of K–12 schools. A sample of principals from schools in the Minneapolis–St. Paul metropolitan area answered survey questions to gauge the impact on their work, their health, their school, and the ways they were handling the pressures of a very tight economy, which had resulted in nearly 13% base budget cuts over a two-year period. Few tend to consider the effects on principals when gauging the impact of declining budgets.

The results suggest that principals like their work and feel good about their performance. Despite the many pressures they face, workplace relations remain intact. There is a resiliency to those leading and working in schools. However, we also learned that faculty and staff morale appears to be declining, that the health of principals has been affected by the continual pressures they face, and that key challenges like making reforms and providing services to students are intensifying.

The situation is so dynamic with no end of budget declines in sight that a new reality is emerging for those serving as principals. Everyone is working harder with less resources; cuts being levied always impact students, teachers, and classrooms (despite the claims to the contrary made by those levying the cuts); the level of negativity aimed at principals is rising; and stress appears to be growing. Facing cutbacks is not new, but the current crisis is more severe than those of the recent past, and few are well prepared for dealing with the outcomes. There are no simple solutions for principals, and the fear is that things will get worse before they return to a more familiar normal.

While the overall results imply that principals are finding ways to hang in and cope with the intense situations they face, what we labeled as disturbing findings suggest that continued stress from working in such an environment may have a significant negative effect on our nation's school leaders. As one principal noted in the comments shared with us, "When is it too much? It would be nice to know what the breaking point is . . . when can we say UNCLE!!!"

These coping tools present some helpful reminders to administrators that leaders should adopt a positive, can-do approach; maintain transparency and openness in communications; and balance work and personal time to strengthen their capacities not only to cope but also to grow in their ability to lead. Leaders who cope well in tough times will likely feel they are acting in the best interests of the organization and be true to their heart in carrying out decisions (Ginsberg & Davies, 2007).

And beyond the school administration, district leaders should realize the importance of principals' morale—and their mental health. Without effective professional development for our school leaders, we may lose them. Life and work are about personal experience and human growth, in better developing and retaining this—and the next—generation of leaders for our schools.

REFERENCES

Behn, R. D. (1980). Leadership for cut-back management: The use of corporate strategy. *Public Administration Review, 40,* 613–620.

Biller, R. P. (1980). Leadership tactics for retrenchment. *Public Administration Review, 40,* 605–609.

Bombyk, M. J., & Chernesky, R. H. (1985). Conventional cutback leadership and the quality of the workplace: Is beta better? *Administration in Social Work, 9,* 47–56.

Caruso, D. R., & Salovey, P. (2004). *The emotionally intelligent manager: How to develop and use the four key emotional skills of leadership.* San Francisco, CA: Jossey-Bass.

Charan, R., & Colvin, G. (2001). Managing for the slowdown. *Fortune, 143,* 78–88.

Clark, K. (2009). Budget cuts take toll on education. *U.S. News and World Report.* Retrieved August 19, 2009 at www.usnews.com/articles/education/best-colleges/2009/08/19/budget-cuts-take-toll-on-education.html.

Conley, S., Gould, J., & Levine, H. (2010). Support personnel: Characteristics and importance. *Journal of Educational Administration, 48,* 309–326.

Coombs, W. T. (1999). *Ongoing crisis communication: Planning, managing, and responding.* Thousand Oaks, CA: Sage.

Ellerson, N. M., & McCord, R. S. (2009). *One year later: How the economic downturn continues to impact school districts.* Arlington, VA: American Association of School Administrators.

Ginsberg, R., & Davies, T. G. (2007). *The human side of leadership: Navigating emotions at work.* Westport, CT: Praeger.

Goleman, D., Boyatzis, R. E., & McKee, A. (2002). *Primal leadership: Realizing the power of emotional intelligence*. Boston: Harvard Business School Press.

Hickman, J. R., & Crandall, W. R. (1997). Before disaster hits: A multifaceted approach to crisis management. *Business Horizons*, 75–79.

Hopkins, G. (2008). Thought leader: Leading in an economic downturn. *New Zealand Management, 55*, 21.

Ihejirika, M. (2010). Devastating layoffs loom in school districts. *Chicago Sun-Times*. Retrieved March 28, 2010 from www.suntimes.com/news/education/2126210,CST-NWS-skuls28.article.

Johnson, N., Oliff, P., & Williams, E. (March 8, 2010). An update on state budget cuts. Center on Budget and Policy Priorities. Retrieved March 30, 2010 from www.cbpp.org/cms/?fa=view$id=1214.

Kash, T. J., & Darling, J. R. (1998). Crisis management: Prevention, diagnosis and intervention. *Leadership & Organization Development Journal, 19*, 179–186.

Leaman, A. (October, 28, 2008). Managing in the downturn. *Business Week* Online, 14.

Levine, C. H. (1978). Organizational decline and cutback management. *Public Administration Review, 38*, 316–325.

Levine, C. H. (1979). More on cutback management: Hard questions for hard times. *Public Administration Review, 39*, 179–183.

Maxwell, L. A. (2010). K–12 cuts loom again as states' fiscal woes continue. *Education Week*. Retrieved March 31, 2010 from www.edweek.org/ew/articles/2010/03/03/23budgets.h29.html.

McTighe, J. J. (1979). Management strategies to deal with shrinking resources. *Public Administration Review, 39*, 86–90.

Miller, D. (2006). Organizational pathology and industrial crisis. In D. Smith & D. Elliott (Eds.), *Key readings in crisis management: Systems and structures for prevention and recovery* (pp. 75–83). London: Routlege, Taylor & Francis Group.

Preble, J. F. (1997). Integrating the crisis management perspective into the strategic management process. *Journal of Management Studies, 34*, 769–791.

Richman, L. S., & Davis, J. E. (1995). Managing through a downturn. *Fortune, 132*, 59–64.

Robert, B., & Lajtha, C. (2002). A new approach to crisis management. *Journal of Contingencies and Crisis Management, 10*, 181–191.

Rockefeller Institute's State Revenue Flash. (February 23, 2010). Retrieved from www.rockinst.org.

Sapriel, C. (2003). Effective crisis management: Tools and best practice for a new millennium. *Journal of Communication Management. 7*, 348–355.

Smith, D. (2006). Beyond contingency planning: Towards a model of crisis management. In D. Smith & D. Elliott (Eds.), *Key readings in crisis management: Systems and structures for prevention and recovery* (pp. 147–158). London: Routledge, Taylor and Francis Group.

Smith, D., & Elliott, D. (2006). *Key readings in crisis management: Systems and structures for prevention and recovery*. London: Routledge, Taylor and Francis Group.

Stern, E., & Sundelius, B. (2002). Crisis management Europe: An integrated regional research and training program. *International Studies Perspectives, 3*, 71–78.

Sullivan, N. (2008). Maintain morale in a downturn. Employee Benefits. Retrieved March 21, 2010 at www.employeebenefits.co.uk/cgi-bin/item.cgi?id=7544.

Chapter Five

Routines, Rituals, and Revival

Sharon Conley, Terrence E. Deal,
and Ernestine K. Enomoto[1]

School leaders entering new job assignments are often puzzled by the routines they encounter—the everyday patterns of behavior that persist even when they seem counterproductive. Typically, one of the first acts of new leaders is changing these routines to get things done with greater efficiency and effectiveness. These leaders are often unaware that they may be tampering with rituals that form the cultural glue, bonding the organization to its history, values, and practices.

Attentiveness to both routines and rituals can prevent backlashes and create opportunities for revival and revitalization by sensitively redefining old ways. A case study of how incoming leadership made changes in well-established school attendance practices illustrates how this process is possible.

Every organization is replete with routinized activity, "repetitive, recognizable patterns of interdependent actions, involving multiple actors" (Feldman & Pentland, 2003, p. 96). Think of McDonald's, where putting together a Big Mac or frying French fries is tightly regulated and done repetitively and automatically. These routines may be established by formal policies and procedures or might simply evolve as people learn how to get their work done.

While providing security, stability, and uniformity, organizational routines can also become a mechanism for change. Feldman (2000) proposed that members within an organization would respond to making or resisting proposed alterations in regular procedures by initiating repairs of existing routines or opting to expand or enhance what currently exists. We have proposed in earlier writing that such change can bring about more fundamental reform in work culture and ethos (Conley & Enomoto, 2005).

Looking at organizational routines through a symbolic lens reveals a deeper level of redundant action. Routines become a historically rooted activity with meaning—communicating and reinforcing an organization's ideals and values (Feldman, 2000, p. 622). According to Bolman and Deal (1984; 2008), routines may be considered rituals when they become important more for what they express intrinsically than for what they produce. They can provide "order and meaning that help to bind an organization together" (Bolman & Deal, 1984, pp. 162–63).

Organizational routines become rituals when they take on symbolic or expressive functions. For example, the recitation of the Pledge of Allegiance at the start of the school day is a routine that becomes a ritual, enacting patriotism. The entire routine at the beginning of the school day—students forming a line outside the door, teacher greeting them, taking attendance, and gathering them into a semicircle for recitation—binds the class together as a cohesive group as much as it focuses students on instruction. One implication of a symbolic view is that the introduction of changes to routines should be undertaken carefully, while considering the meaning; that is, the "thoughts, feelings, and action" people experience (Feldman, 2000, p. 622).

THE INTERPLAY OF ROUTINES AND RITUALS

Although rituals and routines are different, the line between them is often fuzzy. An action can provide uniformity, accountability, and security while, at the same time, reinforcing values and bonding people in common purpose. Roll call in police departments makes sure all officers are on duty while preparing them mentally for their shift. Rituals can also knit people in a shared cultural union while simultaneously enhancing the tangible outcomes of their work. Cockpit checklists in an airliner assure that all systems are in order while at the same time bonding the flight crew together, preparing them for the awesome responsibility of holding human lives in their hands.

Routines can become ritualized; rituals can then lose their meaning by becoming routine. A new superintendent ended his first presentation to the district's teachers and staff by lighting the "lamp of learning," a small bronze oil lamp on the lectern. No one mentioned it afterward. The next year, he ended with the same closing gesture. Again, no comments. Prior to the third opening he was stopped by several people who asked, "You are going to ignite our spirit again this year, aren't you?" The superintendent's opening routine was now a shared cultural ritual.

Just as often, rituals can become routinized, stripping the historically anchored, repetitive action of its meaning and significance. In the 1960s, the Catholic Church changed its liturgy from Latin to English. Rationally, the switch made sense since most parishioners did not understand Latin. But symbolically, many members felt cut off and became profoundly upset by the switch. Richard Rodriguez's reaction in *Hunger of Memory* (1983) describes his reaction to the change in the Catholic Church.

> Now I go to mass every Sunday. Old habits persist. But it is an English mass I attend, a ritual of words. A ritual that seeks to feed my mind and would starve my somewhat metaphorical soul. The mass is less ornamental; it has been 'modernized,' tampered with, demythologized, deflated. . . . But now that I no longer live as a Catholic in a Catholic world, I cannot expect the liturgy—which reflects and cultivates my faith—to remain what it was. I will continue to go to the English mass. I will go because it is my liturgy. I will, however, often recall with nostalgia the faith I have lost. (pp. 101, 107)

In this chapter, we present a case of how the leadership in a California high school altered the attendance monitoring practices to address increased student absences and tardies. The case illustrates how a school leader entering a new job assignment acted to change an existing routine and, in doing so, also changed schoolwide ritual.

RIVERA HIGH SCHOOL

Our initial research in this study began in 1999 as an investigation of routines in various school organizations (Conley & Enomoto, 2005). Included were a high school, a private international school, and a central state office, each with routines in place for different operations. Focusing on the high school, we later documented changes in student attendance routines at Rivera High (all names of school and people are pseudonyms). For more on the research, see Conley and Enomoto (2005; 2009) and Enomoto and Conley (in press).

Located in a semirural community of 40,000 in central California, Rivera is one of two comprehensive high schools in the district. Rivera had an enrollment of approximately 1,150 students in grades 9 through 12, composed of 60% Caucasian, 26% Hispanic, 7% African-American, 5% Asian-Pacific Islander, and 2% Native American. Approximately 40% of the student body was of a minority background, and 18% qualified for free or reduced lunch subsidies. The school's surrounding community was in flux, as the size of the school-age population was growing and student demographics were shifting (*High School Accountability Report Card,* 2003–04).

Rivera employed 70 teachers, almost all fully credentialed. Although the faculty had been stable for over a decade, recent teacher retirements had resulted in a turnover of about one third of the staff. A number of the new teachers were former students returning as teachers. Overall, the school enjoyed an excellent reputation for maintaining a strong academic focus with exemplary programs in ocean sciences and technology. The school was ranked as a top performer according to California's Academic Performance Index.

Initially, we focused on the new way of monitoring attendance instituted by the new principal Hank Peterson and his administrative team. The new leadership replaced the attendance monitoring and follow-up procedures in order to reduce the workload of attendance clerks and administrators in the main office. Peterson also wanted to increase the flow of information from the classroom and to place teachers in direct contact with students' families.

We revisited the school after Peterson retired and a new administration under Ben Nelson took charge. We were interested in seeing what had happened in the transition and whether new challenges of taking attendance confronted the incoming administration (Conley & Enomoto, 2009). A third change in the (attendance) routine occurred when the school district mandated the implementation of a computerized system for recording student attendance (Enomoto & Conley, 2007). We did more to broaden our inquiry during Mr. Nelson's tenure and were able to contact a range of teachers, staff, and district personnel for interviews.

When a third administration came to Rivera, we examined additional modifications in the tardy monitoring routine by reviewing school reports, collecting artifacts, and conducting yet another round of interviews (Enomoto & Conley, in press). As the study spanned multiple administrations over seven years, we were able to take a long-term view of changes in the attendance routine.

Altering Rivera's Attendance Routine

Hank Peterson was hired from out of state. By his second year, he had formed a strong administrative team that included a new assistant principal (AP) with whom he had worked before and a dean of students who had previously taught English at the high school. According to one teacher, the team was so cohesive that "a conversation with one was a conversation with all." The leadership sought to change the routines, modeling some after the high school where Mr. Peterson and Ms. Eve Adams, the AP, had previously served. Attendance monitoring was one of their prime targets.

The attendance procedures in place at Rivera had been routine for years. Teachers reported absences and tardiness to the office; the staff consolidated the information daily. If a student had excessive absences or tardy notices, either the AP or the dean of students would meet with the student or contact the parents. Meanwhile, the office was reporting and making contacts with parents.

With a growing student population and changes in community demographics, the number of truancies increased and created more work for administrators and office staff. Peterson and his administrative team found this unacceptable. According to Adams, "We're getting to the point where our enrollment keeps increasing each year and we're not getting extra help." She noted reductions in staffing in the student career center, and the office was not able to follow up with students' families. "We're not able to call every day every kid who is absent to get those kids back to school."

As a result, Peterson introduced a new routine for taking attendance and monitoring tardies in his second year as principal. Called "3-6-9," the procedure made the teachers responsible for telephoning parents or guardians when a student received three, six, or nine tardy notices (tardies) in class. Rather than the administrators, teachers were to be "first responders" to contact parents and give notice of absences and tardies. Teachers were also responsible for generating the discipline referrals for students with excessive violations (i.e., being three, six, or nine times tardy). These discipline referrals triggered the administrator's involvement with the student and parents for handling progressively greater penalties or consequences.

Dan Richards, a veteran science teacher, described 3-6-9 in this way.

> As a teacher you need to make a contact with the parent if the student has three tardies. [Before the routine was in place,] you could contact a parent if you wanted. . . .You would sign [tardy] slips to give students a lunch detention. The slips would then go to the office.

But Richards admitted, that the prior system "created a lot of work for the office staff." He stated, "With 3-6-9, teachers are more involved [in attendance monitoring]."

The reception from the teachers was mixed. Richards said, "Some teachers did [3-6-9] religiously, while others did not bother with regular enforcement." Another AP, Mike Garcia, affirmed, "some people weren't calling home [while] some people were." There appeared to be substantial variation in implementing the 3-6-9 procedure. Garcia continued:

"Some teachers were writing kids tardy when they were already seated but had [left] their seats to throw away a piece of paper. The teacher could say, 'You weren't in your seat when the bell rang, so that was a tardy.' Other teachers weren't enforcing the policy whatsoever; a student could walk in late. For other teachers, if a student was running toward a classroom, making a valiant effort, they wouldn't write them as being tardy. So 3-6-9 wasn't uniformly [enforced]."

According to Garcia, it was important for teachers to mark attendance and tardies consistently because administration was "supposed to make sure that things [were] applied uniformly when [issuing] consequences" to students. But he went on to say that forcing all teachers to comply was not "worth falling on our sword for. . . . We'd probably be better spending our time making sure that quality instruction is happening in the classroom."

Some veteran teachers attempted to hinder the 3-6-9 procedure by asking new teachers not to participate. Ben Nelson, veteran teacher and later administrator, said,

> We have teachers who have been on this site for 30 years. These teachers are so used to the routines that they have established for themselves, it is very hard for them to adapt to new routines that are established by new administrators, especially with relatively high turnover rate in administrators, particularly [the] assistant principals [APs].

But as the veteran teachers retired and new teachers replaced them, the resistance lessened and the new attendance routine took hold. The next administration taking over after Principal Peterson's retirement continued to refine attendance and tardy monitoring because time spent in class was viewed as being directly related to student achievement.

THEORETICAL FRAMEWORK

Routines

Organizational routines within a school can influence what occurs on a daily basis. Attendance taking offers a good example of a school organizational routine because it occurs in a similar fashion throughout most secondary schools in the United States. Habitually enacted, the routine typically begins at the start of the class period with the teacher recording which students are present or absent. If students arrive after the bell has rung, they are marked tardy. The teacher reports this information on attendance and tardies to the administrative office, where data are consolidated in some fashion by attendance clerks. If a student is consistently absent or tardy, his or her parents are notified and consequences are administered accordingly.

An individual action, when repeated routinely, serves to control and coordinate the behavior of individuals in the organization. This repetition not only shapes what ideally should be done but also what people enact (Feldman, 2000; Feldman & Pentland, 2003). When new teachers are oriented to the school, they are instructed in how and when attendance is taken, what consequences result, and what is expected of teachers in communicating with parents. Their specific attendance-taking practices may vary somewhat with the particular person, place, and-or circumstance.

However, these routinized actions, taken collectively, contribute to the organization's stability and performance as individuals employ routines to take action even when lacking time, attention, information, and certainty (Cohen & Bacdayan, 1994). For individuals, established routines can be comfortable, freeing them from unnecessary details and potentially lessening job stress (Deal, 2007).

That people take comfort from the routines of work is one reason for their persistence. For example, Deal (2007) recounted that a large accounting firm computerized its records to reduce the amount of time required to process forms by hand. The sponsors of the change were surprised when the new system appeared to take more time than the old one. A closer inspection revealed that clerical staff continued to record information by hand and then entered it into computers. Keeping two sets of books eliminated sacrificing old ways but undermined the rationale for making the procedural changes.

At the same time, individuals within the organization can change routines as they reflect upon and respond to their work. According to Feldman (2000), organization members act as independent agents drawing upon their ideals, values, interpretations, feelings, and behavior to take action. In a university housing study, Feldman found that people often made plans and acted upon those plans, the outcomes of which would determine what could happen next.

They might choose to *repair* a routine that did not achieve its intended result or caused something undesirable. Or they could *expand* some routine or might *strive* toward a better or even different result. With multiple actors involved in interpreting routines, this "cycle of plans, actions, outcomes, and ideals" creates a continuous yet dynamic sequence of change within the organization (Feldman, 2000, p. 622).

Feldman (2000) also suggested that change may not be externally generated: for example, it could be caused by a financial crisis or an industry innovation. Rather, change is found within the organization and is internally generated by individuals responding to various outcomes (Feldman, 2000). Routines within the organization could be likened to the "grammar" of an organization (Pentland, 1995; Pentland & Rueter, 1994). Those who know the organization's "grammar" can create new and different ways to express what they mean. They might generate new words, create different sentence constructions, and even introduce new grammatical rules to put words together.

"Unpacking" a routine and how it changes, Pentland and Feldman (2005) contended, means examining all aspects that comprise the internal structure of the routine (p. 801). The researchers contrasted the performative and ostensive aspects of routines as well as their artifacts. The *performative* aspect of a routine reflects actions taken "by specific people, at specific times, and in specific places" (p. 795), as in the actions carried out by individual teachers taking attendance but varying how they do it from day to day.

By contrast, the *ostensive* aspect relates to the generalized pattern guiding an individual's performances, as for example, the directives given when a computerized attendance data system replaces a paper-and-pencil system. While expectations of taking attendance are the same, the directives to do it are different because of the automation (Enomoto & Conley, 2007). The *artifacts* of a routine (i.e., its physical manifestations) codify any routine in the form of standard operating procedures, checklists, forms (such as an attendance "bubble sheet"), and/or occasionally computers and the physical layout of space.

Leaders may find it valuable to understand the routinized or habitual actions, often taken for granted as they attempt to reform and revitalize their organizations. They should note, however, that individual members will act independently on what is happening based upon all aspects, the performative as well as the ostensive ones directing what they do on a daily basis.

Rituals

Routines become *rituals* when they are important more for what they express than for what they actually produce. A specific routine, conceived of as a ritual activity, might convey a sense of order, clarity, and predictability that can be important for the group when dealing with issues or problems that are highly complex, mysterious, or randomly occurring. Bolman and Deal (2008) suggested that Indian rain dances and the Thanksgiving celebration of the Pilgrims represent efforts to invoke supernatural assistance in the critical but unpredictable process of raising crops.

Likewise, individuals might engage in specific routines to ensure successful outcomes. Workers at Wal-Mart routinely begin their shifts with a company cheer and light stretching. "Wal-Mart's rituals may seem like corporate Kool-Aid—spirited at best, cultist at worst—yet they enable the company to organize hundreds of workers around a common goal: operate a store more than three times the size of the White House" (Rosenbloom, 2009, p. 6).

Martin (2002) documented varied kinds of ritualized activities that were for different purposes. For example, in a manufacturing company, a carefully sequenced "pour time" activity ended a crucial stage of the foam production process (Rifkin, cited in Martin, 2002, p. 66). The sequence redirected workers' attention away from the dangerous production process toward a dramatic spectacle of orderly activity. According to Martin (2002), "pour time" illustrated a *renewal* ritual that sought to resolve one set of problems while drawing attention away from another.

Other types of rituals discussed by Martin (2002) convey different meanings for members within the organization. *Initiation* rituals involve the indoctrination of new employees to "the ways things are done here." *Enhancement* rituals express recognition of good performance, as in hosting awards to acknowledge outstanding teachers. By contrast, *degradation* rituals chastise or even expel poor performers from the organization. Finally, *integration* rituals provide opportunities that strengthen interpersonal ties and team building within the organization, as the year-end holiday office parties or seasonal softball games.

For institutionalized organizations like schools, maintaining rituals may be particularly important for the meanings they convey (Bolman & Deal, 2008; Deal, 2007). For example, homecoming activities might signal the final matchup between two high school rivals coupled with welcoming back the alumni who have witnessed that competition for many generations. The rituals and routines of the high school's homecoming sustain the tradition, reinforcing the belief in the school and its accomplishments, athletics as well as academic.

Changes in rituals should be undertaken carefully, considering the meanings and importance of rituals to the organization (Deal, 2007). While a new routine or ritual might be seen as a progressive activity, implementing such a change can disrupt the status quo and generate a strong counterattack from teachers, parents, and students. Because change in culture can be "difficult, time-consuming, and highly anxiety provoking," a leader needs to understand how to get at the deeper levels of the organizational culture (Schein, 1992, p. 27). She or he would need to consider the assumptions made at the various levels of the culture (i.e., organizational artifacts that are visible, espoused values, and underlying, taken-for-granted beliefs) and the potential anxiety that might be created when these three levels are challenged.

Leaders need to recognize where the organization is in its evolution. If newly formed, the leader as founder can create the organizational culture as Sam Walton, the Wal-Mart founder, did by drawing from what he saw at a South Korean tennis-ball factory in the 1970s (Rosenbloom, 2009). But during organizational midlife, the organizational culture is embedded in its structure and major processes; thus it would be more difficult for the leadership to decipher and change the culture (Schein, 1992, p. 314). The appointment of new leadership can initiate change as they bring in their own people and replace the establishment.

According to Dyer (1986), if the conflict between old and new is successfully abated and the new leader is credited for its resolution, then new assumptions take shape and are reinforced by a different set of patterns and routines. This phenomena is what we examined in our case study of the attendance reporting and tardy monitoring routine in Rivera High School.

DISCUSSION

Under Principal Hank Peterson's leadership, the routine of attendance taking and tardiness monitoring did change at Rivera High School. What had been administrator driven became attendance taking and tardy monitoring, with teachers now placed in charge as "first responders" in addressing students with excessive absenteeism and tardy notices. The following were factors contributing to that change.

First, environmental forces such as community demographic changes and more students at the high school increased the number of attendance violations and resulting citations, giving the administrators and office staff more work. According to Feldman's (2000) typology, the change response was a necessary *repair* to address the excessive workload for administrators, which was justified by the need for more efficiency and streamlining administrative operations.

Second, a new leadership team had been hired, bringing in new personnel with different ideas. But it should be noted that the principal did not initiate changes immediately; rather, he did so in his second year at Rivera. As an outsider, he might have taken time to study and decipher the school organization and its culture before attempting to make changes (Schein, 1992).

Third, the leadership imported a new routine from Principal Peterson's prior school, an action that exemplified how individuals might borrow work routines from other settings (Gersick & Hackman, 1990; Levitt & March, 1988). Hank Peterson had experience with the routine, making it more credible to the teaching staff as a tested school practice. Further, he was supported in implementing the practice by AP Eve Adams, who had been with him at the other school and was therefore familiar with the routine.

Fourth, the 3-6-9 routine produced a new role for teachers, making them more responsible for their own students, having them telephone parents, and write up detentions. The change in routine attempted to strive toward the ideal of having those who were most knowledgeable about students, namely the classroom teachers, being responsible for communicating with parents about student attendance. The label "first responders" also connotes an aura of importance.

Police, fire, and other emergency personnel who arrive on a situation ahead of others hold a special status. Their initial efforts are crucial to a positive outcome, and they receive ample attention. Similarly, teachers who spot problems early and take action immediately are often rewarded personally and recognized publicly. Framing the teachers as a "critical response team" rather than "office workers" gave special meaning to the new routine. Making teachers "first responders" was also in line with the notion that teachers were valued at Rivera as the primary contact in relating to parents and families about student concerns.

Finally, the well-established teaching staff was slowly being replaced by newer, younger teachers. Thus, while the veteran teachers were attempting to resist change, newer teachers were being socialized into different roles based on the notion that they should be more involved with contacting parents and guardians. These changes signaled that the new administration under Principal Peterson was able to create a different role for teachers.

As a result of these factors, school leadership could alter "repetitive, recognizable" patterns of actions to repair what did not work, expand positive outcomes, and strive toward new ideals or targets (Feldman & Pentland, 2003, p. 96). The routine of attendance taking and tardiness monitoring expressed "ideals, values, actions, and behaviors" (Feldman, 2000, p. 622), indicating that routines can also become rituals. That Principal Peterson was able to successfully alter the routine and reorient teachers to their new roles illustrates how leadership could revitalize and reform a school's practices, despite teacher resistance.

CONCLUSION

Efforts to reform public education have compiled, at best, a spotty record of change. Billions of dollars have been spent with very little impact on schools and classrooms. One reason is that any significant change requires altering organizational routine and ritual. Existing routines provide comfort and confidence. Doing something over and over again gives people a sense of security and a feeling of competence and being in control. One of the best predictors of a successful surgical outcome is how many times the surgeon has performed the procedure. Altering an organizational routine produces feelings of incompetence, being out of control, and insecurity.

As such, people resist changes in routine for good reason: they want to be in control of their work and enjoy the rewards of mastery. One of the prime ingredients of successful change is training, which provides both new skills and psychological support to reduce the feelings of insecurity and incompetence that come in new roles. But many organizations, schools included, do not provide adequate resources for the development of new skills and the psychological support for the new skill adoption.

Changing an organizational routine is not easy, but changing a ritual is even more difficult because rituals are embedded in cultural tradition. In enacting a ritual, people reinforce shared beliefs and values and bond with each other in a symbolic union. When a ritual changes, it undercuts a group's meaning and sense of significance. Earlier, we looked at Rodriguez's reaction to the Catholic Church's switch from Latin to English in the traditional liturgy. The same sentiments arise among educators, often unconsciously, when reform efforts replace deeply rooted cultural patterns.

For new ways to take hold, people need to let go of their timeworn, customary attachments. The most effective bridge for ritual change is the use of "transitional rituals" to help people mourn symbolic ties and celebrate the new norms of behavior (Bolman & Deal, 2003, p. 393). Very seldom do schools convene rites to transform foreign practices into new traditions.

New leaders do not always recognize the importance of routines and rituals. Instead, they may operate according to the classic rational approach, assuming that organizational members will adopt the leader's directives as stated. Our case explains how one leader enacted change with attention to routines and rituals. The leader chose to wait one year prior to enacting change, thereby studying organizational ritual prior to altering routine. Furthermore, the change in routine enacting recognized the meaning of the teachers' role within the organization by making them first responders. This preferred role for the teachers became imbued with the force of ritual.

The primary purpose of this chapter is to help people see below the surface of policy changes to reveal the subtle shifts of organizational culture required to meet challenges. For decades, we have attempted to improve schools. The main target has been structure, standards, and standardized testing. We have mostly overlooked the training and the intangible aspects of schools that make any organization thrive. Now is a good time for leaders to lift the veneer and attend to the renewal and revival of important educational routines and rituals.

REFERENCES

Bolman, L. G., & Deal, T. E. (1984). *Modern approaches to understanding managing organizations.* San Francisco: Jossey-Bass.

Bolman, L. G., & and Deal, T. E. (2003). *Reframing organizations: Artistry, choice, and leadership.* San Francisco: Jossey-Bass.

Bolman, L. G., & and Deal, T. E. (2008). *Reframing organizations: Artistry, choice, and leadership.* (2nd ed.). San Francisco: Jossey-Bass.

Cohen, M., & Bacdayan, P. (1994). Organizational routines are stored as procedural memory: Evidence from a laboratory study. *Organization Science, 5*(4), 554–568.

Conley, S., & Enomoto, E. K. (2005). Routines in school organizations: Creating stability and change. *Journal of Educational Administration, 43*(1), 9–21.

Conley, S., & Enomoto, E. K. (2009). Organizational routines in flux: A case study of change in recording and monitoring student attendance. *Education and Urban Society, 41*, 364–386.

Deal, T. (2007). Sustainability of the status quo. In B. Davies (Ed.), *Developing sustainable leadership* (pp. 87–96). London: Paul Chapman.

Dyer, W. G. Jr. (1986). *Culture change in family firms*. San Francisco: Jossey-Bass.

Enomoto, E. K., & Conley, S. (2007). Harnessing technology for school accountability. A case study of implementing a management information system. *Planning and Changing, 38,* 164–180.

Enomoto, E. K., & Conley, S. (in press). Changing the guard: How different school leaders change organizational routines. *Journal of School Leadership.*

Feldman, M. S. (2000). Organizational routines as a source of continuous change. *Organization Science, 11*(6), 611–629.

Feldman, M. S., & Pentland, B. T. (2003). Reconceptualizing organizational routines as a source of flexibility and change. *Administrative Science Quarterly, 48,* 94–118.

Gersick, C. J. G., & Hackman, J. R. (1990). Habitual routines in task-performing groups. *Organizational Behavior and Human Decision Processes, 47,* 65–97.

High School Accountability Report Card, 2003–04. System documentation.

Levitt, B., & March, J. G. (1988). Organizational learning. *Annual Review of Sociology, 14,* 319–340.

Martin, J. (2002). *Organizational culture: Mapping the terrain*. Thousand Oaks, CA: Sage.

Pentland, B. T. (1995). Grammatical models of organizational processes. *Organizational Science, 6*(5), 541–556.

Pentland, B. T., & Feldman, M. S. (2005). Organizational routines as a unit of analysis. *Industrial and Corporate Change, 5,* 793–815.

Pentland, B. T., & Rueter, H. H. (1994). Organizational routines as grammars of action. *Administrative Science Quarterly, 39*(3), 484–510.

Rifkin, C. (1985). *Rituals in organizations*. Unpublished manuscript, Stanford University, Stanford, CA.

Rodriguez, R. (1983). *The hunger of memory: The education of Richard Rodriguez*. New York: Bantam.

Rosenbloom, S. (2009, December 20). My initiation at Store 5476. *New York Times,* December 20, 2009, 1, 6.

Schein, E. H. (1992). *Organizational culture and leadership, 2nd ed*. San Francisco: Jossey-Bass.

Chapter Six

Mentoring Latina/Latino Leaders

Kenneth R. Magdaleno

It is an illusion that the hearts of men and women can be transformed while the social structure which makes those hearts sick is left intact and unchanged.

—Paolo Freire

The above quote points to the necessity of transforming social structures in society that are not meeting the needs of its people. In 1972, Rudolfo Acuña wrote in *Occupied America: The Chicano's Struggle toward Liberation* that the goal of the "Chicano movement" was not to become simply another conquering force retaking America but instead to aspire to equity for all. Acuña (1972) emphasized that the "great humanistic and historical task of the oppressed is to liberate themselves and their oppressors as well" (p. 5).

However, currently in California, as in much of the United States, despite the growing diversity of its population, the ethnic composition of state and local educational leadership administration systems has remained virtually unchanged since Acuña's observation in 1972. While also accumulating and sharing decision-making power, Latina and Latino educators are challenged to increase their presence and roles as leaders in the educational administrative ranks.

Thus, after years of tenacity and a push for equality, Latina and Latino leaders in education continue to remain marginalized. Disparities in their leadership representation at the site, district, and state levels persist, largely owing to the sparse numbers of Latinas and Latinos selected for site and district leadership positions. In California, approximately 49% of the over 6 million students attending California schools are Latina or Latino (California Department of Education [CDE], 2009). Yet recent demographic data indicate that Latina and

Latino administrators serving as public school educational leaders total only 5,002 or 17.9% of California's school leaders (CDE, 2009).

In 2004, the percentage of Latina and Latino education administrators was 15.4%, indicating a slight increase of 2.3% in the last five years (CDE, 2009). For Latina and Latino leaders, access to information, visibility, and prospects to demonstrate competence are examples of opportunity dimensions that are not sufficiently available to them (Dreher & Cox, 1996) even to this day. The establishment of an administrator mentoring system composed of competent, credible, and experienced Latino educational leaders mentoring each other, as well as junior administrators, is one way of addressing the equity and access issues.

This chapter examines some rationales for creating an administrator mentoring system for Latino leaders generally, including specific rationales drawn from the author's experience in designing a Latino mentoring system in California in 2004. The chapter begins with a brief historical background of the Latino culture, followed by details regarding the cultural and social assets of Latinos. Additional background on the issues of culture and power is provided in turn, followed by the topics of Latinos as influential positive leaders and mentors. The chapter concludes by illustrating the importance of role modeling by present-day Latino educational leaders for students in public schools in California and elsewhere.

THE LATINO CULTURE

Understanding the Latino experience is key to realizing and appreciating Latinos in the United States. Present-day Latinos, and their ancestors, arrived in the United States from at least 21 different countries. A good number of Latinos are "mestizos," persons of mixed blood derived from Native American Indian, African, and European roots, often bilingual, speaking both Spanish and English. Some are dark in complexion, and still others have a light skin color. Coming in all sizes and shapes, many describe themselves as Latinos; others use the terms Chicanos, Boricua, Cubans, Dominicans, Ecuadorians, or Hispanics.

Latinos who trace their heritage in the United States to the first Spanish settlements are numerous, especially in California, Arizona, New Mexico, and Texas. Other Latinos are the descendants of Mexicans who chose to stay in the United States after the Mexican-American War (1846–1848). Many of them are first- and second-generation U.S. citizens fleeing economic or political upheavals in Latin America, such as the Mexican Revolution, the Cuban Revolution, or the civil wars in Nicaragua, El Salvador, the Dominican Republic, and Guatemala (Abalos, 2002), along with today's difficult economic climate.

While some Latinas and Latinos have achieved the American dream, many have not, and thus remain on the lower rungs of society's ladder (Abalos, 2002, p. 2). To Latinas and Latinos, the American dream encompasses much more than economic prosperity. It symbolizes personal advancement, the ability to provide a better life for their children, and the individual pursuit of liberty and justice (see also www.latinoleadership.org). The Latino experience in the United States has also been profoundly shaped by immigration (Suarez-Orozco & Paez, 2002), and a substantial majority of Latinos are either immigrants or the children of immigrants. In many cases, immigrants continue to maintain the language and culture that they brought with them from their mother country.

A recent statistical portrait developed by the Pew Hispanic Center reveals that in 2007, the Hispanic population in the United States totaled 45,378,596. Between 2000 and 2007 Hispanics in the United States increased from 12.5% to 15% of the total population: from 35 million to 45 million. Native-born Hispanics numbered 27,328,758 and foreign-born Hispanics totaled 18,049,838 (Pew, 2007). In response to these quickly changing racial-cultural demographic realities, educators, social scientists, parents, and community representatives have called for changes in school policy and practice.

They have challenged the adequacy of current curricula and teacher training, questioned the racial-cultural composition of the teacher population, and shown concern for the low number of Latina and Latino school administrators in a time of rapid ethnic and demographic transformation (Carter, 2000).

CULTURAL AND SOCIAL ASSETS OF LATINAS AND LATINOS

Gardiner, Enomoto, and Grogan (2000) asserted that the "dominant culture of educational administration is adrocentric, meaning informed by white, male norms" (p. 1). Experiences that Latinas and Latinos face as educational leaders are unlike those of the current dominant educational leadership group, and many of these experiences are a result of stereotypes that have been passed down from one generation to another, often persisting without a sense of the damage such false impressions can cause.

For example, self-confidence, energy, tenacity, risk taking, and a sense of humor are often seen as leadership qualities in the majority culture. However, these same qualities, when exhibited by minorities, are often misconstrued as arrogance, aggressiveness, threatening, nonconformism, and a lack of seriousness (Wilson & Melendez, 1988). A Latina school superintendent described her experience in the following manner (Magdaleno, 2004):

I kind of like to think of it, that we have a lot more to offer than your White male. Because we're working in a White dominant society and we're able to cross the line, kind of swing both ways and we know how to behave and how to perform in a White dominated society. Those are the power brokers. But then again we can go home and be very comfortable in our cultural environment. (p. 56)

Misunderstanding the cultural nuances of specific ethnic groups makes it difficult to gain access to the networks developed by the dominant culture and may result in the placement of barriers. Wilson and Melendez (1988) argued that it is essential for Latino leaders to be placed in mainstream activities to break down these barriers (see also Gutierrez, Castaneda, & Katsinas, 2002).

Guadalupe Figueroa wrote in *A Charla [Informal Conversation] with My Mentor* that an important part of the Latino culture, which helps shape mentoring relationships, is the concept of *respeto,* which in her research cannot be translated simply as "respect." Socialization in Latino communities is based on traditional values of *respeto* for human dignity and values (Figueroa, 2003). In shaping the many aspects of cultural assets for Latinos, familialism is also consistently at the forefront. Familialism (also called *familism* or *familismo*) is a cultural value conveying individuals' strong identification with and attachments to nuclear and extended families, along with strong feelings of loyalty, reciprocity, and solidarity among members of the same family.

This value appears to help protect individuals against stress by providing a natural support system that is primary for mentors and protégés when the value of caring for each other is not considered a duty, but an honor (Marin & Marin, 1991). Latino administrators, desiring to become school district leaders, may gain valuable leadership skills from current superintendents and fellow district leaders who possess these characteristics. As such, Latino cultural values make the development of an administrator mentoring program serving Latina and Latino leaders both valuable and timely.

ACCESS, EQUITY, AND POWER THROUGH MENTORING SUPPORT FOR LATINO LEADERS

Swartz (1997) wrote in *Culture and Power: The Sociology of Pierre Bourdieu,* that a key question stirring Pierre Bourdieu's work is, "How do inequalities of privilege and power persist intergenerationally without conscious recognition and public resistance?"(p. 190). According to Bourdieu, the answer lies in the control and use of cultural resources by individuals and groups to perpetuate positions of privilege and power. Bourdieu believed that the educational system had become the institution most responsible for the transmission of social inequality in modern societies (cited in Swartz, 1997).

"Power comes from the ability to control the definition of situations" (Rosado, 1997, p. 4). The dominant White culture in the State of California presently controls the condition of educational leadership and its decision-making power. If the state of education and its educational leadership are going to improve for Latino leaders, then those in power must be persuaded of the benefits of inclusion. However, until such change takes place, Latinos themselves must continue to develop a strong network of influential decision makers sensitive to the needs of Latino leadership.

A CASE STUDY: THE CALSA MENTORING PROGRAM

Over the last six years, the California Association of Latino School Administrators (CALSA) has implemented an administrative mentoring program for Latino leaders with research accumulating on the success of the program and experiences with administrative mentoring in the state (Magdaleno, 2009). The following section outlines some of the rationales of the mentoring approach and the potential of its use.

As members of a mentoring support program, Latinas and Latinos will teach, lead, support, and further the career interests of other Latina and Latino educational leaders. Concurrently, by providing examples of the value of social and cultural assets, Latinas and Latinos may also persuade members of the dominant culture that the sharing of power is beneficial to all. The development of a mentoring support program for Latino administrators should take advantage of the familial and community characteristics that make Latinos dependent on and supportive of each other.

In the popular press, Stephen R. Covey (1996), author of *The Seven Habits of Successful People*, maintained that the leader of the future is "one who creates a culture or value system based on the principles of service, integrity, fairness, and equity" (Covey, 1996, p. 33). Deal and Prince (2003), writing for the Center for Creative Leadership, stated,

> Thinking about cultural differences around the world isn't just an intellectual exercise for managers working in an increasingly global environment. Being able to communicate effectively across cultural differences, understanding how to negotiate complex social situations, and being familiar with the customs and norms of many cultures are important skills in organizations today. Perhaps even more important than possessing those essential pieces of cultural knowledge is the skill of cultural adaptability—the willingness and ability to recognize, understand, and work effectively across cultural differences. (p. 7)

Proficiency in cultural adaptability helps contemporary managers to build the relationships needed to achieve results in today's global organizations, especially when those relationships are forged across borders and cultures. It enables them to interact effectively with people different from themselves, whether these people work on the next floor or on the other side of the world.

Like many others, California is a state that is becoming more ethnically and culturally diverse—and certainly has become more Latina and Latino. According to Hernandez and Ramirez (2001), because U.S. Latinos already live as a multicultural people within multicultural contexts, they often possess the experiences, cultural knowledge, and skills that cultural adaptability requires.

Latina and Latino leaders who serve as educational leaders are conscious of the obstacles and issues that members of their ethnic group face in leadership roles. For example, as a Latina superintendent expressed it,

> The White man is at the top, not even a White female is up there, and for some reason, the system of public education expects less from the White man than it would from a man of color or a woman, or a woman of color.

A Latina or Latino mentor skilled in the difficulties of serving as a district or site leader is capable of guiding his or her protégés through the racial and gender barriers based on cultural capital gained in his or her personal and professional experiences. Cultural capital refers to factors that provide human societies with the means and adaptations to deal with the natural environment and actively to modify it. It also includes how people view the world and the universe, or cosmology in the sense of Skolimowski's (1981) environmental philosophy and ethics, including religion (Leopold, 1949; Naess, 1989), traditional ecological knowledge (Naess, 1989), and social/political institutions (Ostrom, 1990).

An extraordinary amount of cultural capital is available in the uniqueness of Latinos and Latinas based on the cultural values of family, respect, service, humility, care, and compassion. Such leadership traits are among the values that current Latino leaders and mentors possess and will entrust and pass along to the next generation. Although other ethnicities may also value the same traits, Latinos appear to place more importance on them and less on such leadership qualities as being visionary and inspirational (Hernandez & Ramirez, 2001).

Given that such cultural capital is available in the uniqueness of Latinos and Latinas, a paradigm shift is required in the manner that schools view the value of Latino and Latina leadership as mentors and role models for the coming generation. One Latino superintendent provided his point of view as follows:

> I think the Latino culture may be closer to having an aspect of helping young people find their way, whether it's into manhood or a career. I think that there's

still that . . . there's more of that connection between generations and it may have something to do with the extended family and the fact that many of us, you know it's not just about the immediate family but it's about an extended family. So, I think that we do take a greater interest in nieces and nephews and the next generation coming up.

I think it's one of the reasons that I got involved with juvenile halls that I mentioned to you earlier. I get real concerned when I see that and I have to remind myself of what's there to bring me back here and really charge me up in terms of the importance of the work that we do in K–6. So, I think that when you think of the compadres and the concept of how important that is to Latinos, that you can always call on a compadre to help you do something, to help you with projects and so forth. I think those are aspects of the Latino culture that are strengths for mentoring. (Magdaleno, 2004, p. 79)

What is it about mentoring that can assist Latino leaders in improving their administrative roles? Authors who have written about mentoring often begin the narrative by describing the epic poem *The Odyssey* and the relationship between Mentor, an Ithacan noble and friend of King Odysseus, and Telemachus, the son of King Odysseus.

Mentor, charged with caring for Telemachus, understood that as a mentor, he was expected to invest a significant amount of time and energy in supporting Telemachus. What is often not explained in the above narrative is that eventually, the goddess Athena assumed Mentor's form to guide, protect, and teach Telemachus during his travels. What is also not often explained is that a male and a female together served as mentors. There was much that each could teach Telemachus—and he was the better for it.

Stoddard (1998), in an article titled *Croaks from the Lily Pad: Toward the Provision of a Peer Mentoring Program for Principals,* described the importance of mentoring in school administration: "The mentoring relationship is special because of its entrusting nature. Those being mentored are dependent upon their mentors to help them, protect them, show them the way, and develop more fully their skills and insights" (Sergiovanni & Starratt, cited in Stoddard, 1998, p. 3). The task of the mentor then is to define a unique, trusting relationship with his or her protégé and to fulfill a need unmet by any other relationship (Samier, 2000).

The best mentors are teachers/sages who act to the best of their ability within plain sight of their protégé and who engage in a compassionate and mutual search for wisdom (Bell, 1996). A well-skilled, experienced educator mentoring a less skilled educator can thus be a critical force in determining the retention of new and emerging educational leaders (Stoddard, 1998).

In today's challenging times, as the pool of district and school administrators shrinks and fewer are willing to carry on the role of educational leadership, a new generation of leaders should step forward and serve schools. A mentoring program that supports these new leaders is needed, as opposed to assuming that they will "suck it up" and "be strong" as they struggle to guide schools and districts in the "exhausted loneliness of administration" (Magdaleno, 2009, p. 28). In one answer to this call, CALSA's administrator mentoring program is as of 2010 serving its sixth cohort. In as many years, more than 100 mentors and protégés in total have participated. Each year, the size of the cohort has increased, with the latest serving 20 protégés from 18 different California school districts.

Prospective protégés (assistant principals, principals, directors) must submit an application, along with a letter of support from their district superintendent. Interviews are utilized not only to select participants but also to help establish a mentoring pair designation. Mentors have typically served as principals or superintendents. Protégés and mentors sign a mentoring agreement and a yearlong developmental plan, both of which are reviewed periodically and updated if needed. At least a bimonthly contact is required, and mentors and protégés both agree to commit to the program for two years. After completing this designated period, CALSA administrators work to track protégés' job assignments and career progress (Magdaleno, 2009).

Sustaining an administrator mentoring support program that improves the probability of success for Latina and Latino educational leaders appears essential. The CALSA Administrator Mentoring Program has been diligent in making an effort to connect its protégés with mentors who can be of assistance, as the current leaders navigate the inherent landmines that appear with leadership positions (Magdaleno, 2009).

Learning from mentors who have gone before them and who share significant lessons, experienced through personal interactions, brings added value to program participants and makes position success and sustainability more likely to occur. In addition, cultivating mentoring practices will help to shape a new administrator's perception and understanding of what it means to be an educational leader in a public institution where student demographics are changing rapidly. This experience will bring a greater understanding of racial, cultural, and diversity practices to the educational profession.

Latino administrators are members of an educational system where student and teacher populations are rapidly changing, providing a unique opportunity to make leadership, cultural responsiveness, and equity quickly accessible where it has rarely existed. Solorzano (1998) addressed mentoring and its impact on one's social mobility—or movement through the educational pipeline under the umbrella of what he termed "sponsored mobility." In this process the elites or their agents call on those individuals (mentors) who have the appropriate qualities. Through important social networks and processes like mentoring, people are chosen to move up and into the best positions within the government, corporate world, and academia.

However, merely having the opportunity is not enough. All administrative leaders should be capable and knowledgeable if they are to be successful. With the changing demographics of the state and nation, the power structure is being transformed. All leaders should be ready for that change and understand how certain aspects of leadership are similar; yet they must also see how valuable cultural and racial differences affect those with whom they share the future of education. Studies indicate that mentoring leads to improved administrator job performance and increased job promotion rate, early career advancement, greater upward mobility, higher income, greater job satisfaction, enhanced leadership ability, and perceptions of greater success and influence in an organization (Hill & Bahniuk, 1998).

MENTORING: ANOTHER LOOK

The above case study focuses on mentoring among Latino and Latina educators as a way of addressing equity for all. The current discussion draws on definitions of mentoring in the larger management and organizational literature to provide ideas about the value of mentoring in a long-range career developmental view.

Mentoring is typically defined as a relationship between an experienced person, the mentor, and a less experienced person, the protégé, in which the mentor provides guidance, advice, support, and feedback to the protégé (Haney, 1997). Although mentoring has existed for thousands of years, only in the last thirty years have mentor-protégé relationships received increasing academic and professional attention in and outside of education.

Much initial research in organizations generally focused on "classical mentoring," in which a protégé, more by chance than by merit, found a mentor willing to serve as guide and counselor (Malone, 2001). According to Kogler-Hill, Bahniuk, Dobos, and Rouner (as cited in Kelly & Schweitzer, 1999), mentoring is defined by the nature of the activity when an older, more experienced member assumes a guiding role with a less experienced colleague. Finally, Anderson and Shannon (as cited in Colwell, 1998) offered the definition of mentoring as:

> A nurturing process in which a more skilled or more experienced person, serving as a role model, teaches, sponsors, encourages, counsels, and befriends a less skilled or less experienced person for the purpose of promoting the latter's professional and/or personal development. (p. 40)

Traditionally, mentoring happened spontaneously and/or sporadically in organizations, as experienced people recognized employees who appeared to have the talent necessary to be leaders and began to mentor them (Institute, 1998). However, "a new mentoring paradigm" has emerged, where protégés have more education but still need to learn from mentors' experience and expertise (Institute, 1998). Mentors have been found to provide two major functions: psycho-social support and career/instrumental mentoring function (Bercik, 1994).

Mentoring is thus a way to help new employees learn about organizational culture (Bierema, 1996), to facilitate personal and career growth and development, and to expand opportunities for those traditionally hampered by organizational barriers, such as women and minorities (Gunn, 1995).

The need for mentoring is demonstrated when, for example, the federal government, using regulatory measures, has tried to increase minority numbers in leadership positions but then failed to ensure environments that assure minority promotion and retention. Thomas (2001), in his article *The Truth about Mentoring Minorities: Race Matters,* stated:

> Diversity has become a top priority in Corporate America. Despite the best intentions though, many organizations have failed to achieve racial balance within their executive teams. Some have revolving doors for talented minorities, recruiting the best and the brightest only to see them leave, frustrated and even angered by the barriers they encounter. (p. 98)

Thomas's (2001) study of the progression of racial minorities in three large U.S. corporations suggested that minorities who advance the farthest share one characteristic: a strong network of mentors and corporate sponsors who nurture the professional development of minority leaders. A qualitative questionnaire, distributed to participants at the 2001 Seventh Annual Summer Symposium of the National Community College Hispanic Council, asked participants, "Was there a key experience in your career path that prepared you for your current position, and if so, what was that?" Primary among the three key themes that emerged from the survey was that respondents benefited significantly from quality mentoring experiences (Gutierrez et al., 2002).

Many mentoring programs are geared specifically to women and minorities as a way of helping them break through the "glass ceiling." The term "glass ceiling" has a number of definitions, including that offered by the U.S. Department of Labor as "those artificial barriers based on attitudinal or organizational bias that prevent qualified individuals from advancing upward in their organization" (Powell & Butterfield, 1994, p. 69). This term is used most often when the organization brings in members of the groups affected by the glass ceiling and promotes them through the lower ranks, and in the lower ranks only, on a comparable basis to the most favored group. When members of a group are inclined to leave the organization soon after entering, a "revolving door" rather than a "glass ceiling" occurs.

The personal relationship at the heart of mentoring can be problematic when the mentor and protégé are of different genders, races, or ethnic backgrounds. Researchers disagree over the advantages and disadvantages of matching characteristics in mentoring relationships (Kerka, 1998). Some argue that race and gender should not play a role in mentor selection (Jossi, 1997). However, other research suggests that it may be advantageous for women and non-White men and non-White women to form multiple mentoring relationships involving not only White men but also people of the same gender or racial group (Ibarra, 1992; Thomas, 2001). Whatever the argument is regarding same-race or cross-race mentoring, mentors still need to be sensitive to different cultural perspectives or mentoring will merely perpetuate homogeneous, exclusionary values and culture (Galbraith & Cohen, 1995).

Although mentoring is important to career success, mentors may not be as readily available to women as they are to men (Noe, 1988). In general, both men and women express the same intentions to mentor others; however, women anticipate more problems stemming from this relationship (Ragins & Cotton, 1991). According to Tannen (1990),

> If women speak and hear a language of connection and intimacy, while men speak and hear a language of status and independence, then communication between men and women can be like cross-cultural communication, prey to a clash of conversation styles. Instead of different dialects, it has been said that they would speak different genderlects. (p. 42)

Furthermore, researchers have long recognized that not all persons make suitable mentors, as the best mentors display certain traits, such as the ability to coach, to sponsor, and to serve as role models. But even the most accomplished mentor can fail to connect with a protégé, resulting in a neutral-effect relationship at best (Malone, 2001).

Minimizing the number of neutral-effect mentoring relationships resulted in the development of tools such as the Mentor Identification Instrument that is used to identify those individuals who possess the needed skills and talents to nurture protégés. By distinguishing those best qualified to mentor, this tool can assist school systems interested in creating an effective mentoring program (Geismar, Morris, & Lieberman, 2000).

LATINA AND LATINO LEADERS SERVING
AS POSITIVE ROLE MODELS

Experience with CALSA's mentoring program (and other efforts) allows us to speculate about additional rationales for administrator mentoring. Serving as a role model *is* a significant responsibility for Latina and Latino school administrators. However, they are aware that for Latina and Latino students, the presence of a Latina or Latino educational leader contravenes a history of low expectations. Latina and Latino school educational mentors and protégés, many of whom are the recipients of a history of low expectations, are often the only models of educational success that Latina and Latino students see and can relate to as ethnic role models (Magdaleno, 2009).

Although Latina and Latino leaders are serving more frequently in policy-making positions, role models for Latinas and Latinos in the area of educational leadership are atypical. Students learn the racial and gendered structuring of the culture in which they live by noting the race and gender of adults in different professional positions. Moreover, race- and gender-matched role models may provide young people with a sense of having a place of value and importance in the future (Zirkel, 2002).

Second, school plays a major role in the culture that students develop. Like the family and neighborhood, school affects how students understand and pursue the opportunities that life provides for them. Education delivers an institutional ideology, socializing agents, and an experiential context within which students define and shape the way they think about their personal dreams (Grant & Sleeter, 1988). In fall 2000, a group of minority students gathered in Cleveland, Ohio, under the auspices of the Minority Student Achievement Network. The students at this meeting indicated that to close the racial achievement gap, children need connections to role models and mentors at the earliest grades (American Association of School Administrators, 2000).

The presence of Latina and Latino leaders, serving as administrative role models, can help build and maintain high self-esteem for Latina and Latino students. The academic success of Latina and Latino students is attributable not only to the environments in the schools they attend but also to the relationships they have with teachers and administrators.

Third, Latino faculty and staff will be more active and aspire to leadership positions if they have advocates and role models (Gutierrez et al., 2002). Unfortunately, the low numbers of Latinos in faculty and administrative positions make it difficult to acquire role models and mentors for both students and aspiring leaders in the educational system (Sedlacek & Fuertes, 1993). This inequity in Latina and Latino role models and mentors negatively affects the power structure to such an extent that the lives of Latina and Latino students are also negatively influenced.

Carrillo (2008) noted that research on Latino leadership and mentoring revealed successes as well as challenges, and that factors identified as obstacles included racism, gender bias, and cultural leadership differences (Carrillo, 2008). Perhaps the challenges are best exemplified in this interview,

which took place between the author and a sitting Latino school superintendent while doing research in 2003 (Magdaleno, 2004):

> I mean, a lot of us have grown up with the prejudices around us, and have either
> isolated or insulated ourselves against them. And that has—I mean obviously the
> plus side of that is we survived. The negative side of it is how we react to it, you
> know. So, I think it's important to have fellow Latinos talk about it. "Listen,
> you're running into a racist crowd here. How are you going to compose your-
> self? What are you going to do? What are the things that you've got to be careful
> of?" You know. That "never let them see you sweat kind of attitude." But I think
> we come from the same place. I mean, we come from having—you know—
> endured that, tolerated it to varying degrees—from just plain outright racism—
> to the very covert, "He's a nice guy, but you know . . ." kind of stuff, which puts
> us in our place.
>
> And it's that being put in your place that I think all of us have gone through
> to some degree that allows us, if we're good survivors, to support one another,
> so that we don't become indignant or—I mean, it's there, the racism is there. We
> can't pretend it's not there, but it's like, how do you respond to it, not react?
> How do you respond to it so that it puts you in the driver's seat, as opposed to,
> you know, "I'm not gonna let them do that to me," or whatever. People know—
> people know that's there. It's kinda like it's the bleeding rhino head in the room
> that nobody wants to talk about it, but it's there. (p. 59)

This epigraph by an experienced school superintendent provides insight into
the unique challenges that Latino educational leaders face and the role that a
support system such as mentoring provides.

CONCLUSION

Rudolph Acuña (1972) asserted that the intention of the Chicano people is not
only to liberate themselves but also to liberate the oppressor. Today's scholar-
ship throughout the educational system involves an ongoing conversation in
relation to collaboration whereby the voice and cultural capital of others not
considered part of the mainstream will be valued. Developing a leadership
and mentoring program for Latino educators is most importantly about *fa-
milia* and about being proud of the Latino culture and its value.

Liberation, value, and voice together include school administrators, teachers, and current and future generations of Latino students who look to those
who have traveled the road before them to show the way. As has often been
pointed out, "our children perceive the possibility for themselves in the adults
that are around them." If all that children observe are adults who are treated as
second-class citizens, then they will only see that possibility for themselves.

However, if through mentoring, a group of educational leaders are developed who are confident, competent, and credible, then school children will have real and positive role models who can guide them away from what often seems to be a "dead-end" dropout road and toward a journey of hope and renewal.

Respect, service, humility, care, and compassion in a Latina or Latino leader are personified by Cesar Chavez: the epitome of Latino leadership. In 1976, near the end of a five-year grape strike, Cesar Chavez spoke of the continuation of the struggle for dignity and respect. His words continue to ring true today: "We want sufficient power to control our own destinies. This is our struggle. It's a lifetime job. The work for social change and against social injustice is never ended" (Levy, 1975, p. 538). The issues for Latinas and Latinos in education continue to be equity, access, and power.

Historically, leaders and students of color have been excluded from decision-making positions in the public school system. The millions of Latina and Latino students need role models now who will give them hope for the future. Too many of our children are dropping out of school because of a system that has not valued their social and cultural capital. The system needs people who understand that the Latina and Latino can be the voice for a growing population.

The future of Latinas and Latinos in education is dependent on preparing the next generation of qualified Latina and Latino professionals to become educational leaders. In the 1950s post–World War II era, limited avenues of advancement and upward mobility were open for Latinas and Latinos. From the Chicano movement eras of the 1960s and 1970s, through the 1980s and 1990s to the present, Latinas and Latinos continue to challenge the status quo and become educational change agents across academia.

No doubt new educational leaders will have many issues to address in the 21st century. The politics of working with school boards, growing diversity and the changing demographics of communities, budget problems currently facing many California schools, and the overcrowding of urban schools are all critical areas expected to be dealt with by educational leaders. According to Sergiovanni (1992), successful systems recognize and cultivate collaborative leadership within the many diverse groups of a school district. Latina and Latino school leaders must be trained and mentored to be successful in such an endeavor.

The mentoring program developed in 2004 in partnership with CALSA is one promising avenue for many Latina and Latino school leaders waiting to become a part of the policy-making structure (Magdaleno, 2009). The presence of Latino school leaders able to mentor each other will help make the transition to "shared power" efficient and enduring.

Changing demographics in schools and changing leadership pools require support for these administrative candidates. Targeted mentoring offers a way to retain these leaders and not trap them beneath the "glass ceiling" or send them out through the "revolving door." The CALSA mentoring program offers a promising avenue toward achieving this goal.

REFERENCES

Abalos, D. T. (2002). *The Latino male: A radical redefinition.* Boulder, CO: Lynn Reiner Publishers, Inc.

Acuña, R. (1972). *Occupied America: The Chicano's struggle toward liberation.* New York: Harper and Row.

American Association of School Administrators. (2000). *Districts look to students for clues in closing achievement gap* [Internet]. Retrieved November 12, 2002 from www.aasa.org/publications.

Anderson, E. M., Shannon, A. L. (1988). Toward a conceptualization of mentoring. *Journal of Teacher Education, 39*(1), 38–42.

Bell, C. R. (1996). *Managers as mentors: Building partnerships for learning.* San Francisco: Berret-Koehler Publishers, Inc.

Bercik, J. T. (1994). The principal's role in mentoring. *Streamlined Seminar, 13*(3).

Bierema, L. L. (1996). *How executive women learn corporate culture* [Internet]. ERIC. Retrieved January 26, 2003, from www.ericdigests.net.

California Department of Education. (2009). *State summary: Number of administrators by ethnicity* [Internet]: Educational Demographics Office. Retrieved from www.ed-data.k12.ca.us.

Carrillo, L. (2008). *What obstacles or support mechanisms do Latinas and Latinos encounter in becoming principals and sustaining their leadership positions in California?* Unpublished dissertation, California State University, Fresno.

Carter, R. T. (2000). Reimagining race in education: A new paradigm for education. *Teachers College Record, 102*(5), 864–897.

Colwell, S. (1998). Mentoring, socialization, and the mentor/protégé relationship. *Teaching in Higher Education, 3*(3), 313–325.

Covey, S. R. (1996). *Three roles of the leader in the new paradigm.* San Francisco: Jossey-Bass.

Deal, J. J., & Prince, D. W. (2003). *Developing cultural adaptability: How to work across differences.* Greensboro, NC: Center for Creative Leadership.

Dreher, G. F., & Cox, T. H. (1996). Race, gender, and opportunity: A study of compensation attainment and the establishment of mentoring relationships. *Journal of Applied Psychology, 81*(3), 297–308.

Figueroa, M. G. (2003). A charla with my mentor. *Culture, Society & Praxis, 1*(2), 97–116.

Galbraith, M. W., & Cohen, N. H. (Eds.). (1995). *Mentoring: New strategies and challenges* (Vol. 66). San Francisco: Jossey-Bass.

Gardiner, M. E., Enomoto, E. K., & Grogan, M. (2000). *Coloring outside the lines.* Albany, NY: State University of New York Press.

Geismar, T. J., Morris, J. D., & Lieberman, M. G. (2000). Selecting mentors as principalship interns. *Journal of School Leadership, 10*(3), 233–247.

Grant, C. A., & Sleeter, C. E. (1988). Race, class, and gender and abandoned dreams. *Teachers College Record, 90*(1), 20–40.

Gunn, E. (1995). *Mentoring, the democratic version* [Internet]. ERIC. Retrieved January 26, 2003 from www.ericdigests.net.

Gutierrez, M., Castaneda, C., & Katsinas, S. (2002). Latino leadership in community colleges: Issues and challenges. *Community College Journal of Research and Practice, 26*, 297–314.

Haney, A. (1997). The role of mentorship in the workplace. In M. C. Taylor (Ed.), *Workplace education* (pp. 211–218). Toronto: Culture Concepts.

Hernandez, A., & Ramirez, A. (2001). *Reflecting an American vista: The character and impact of Latino leadership.* Washington DC: National Community for Latino Leadership, Inc.

Hill, S. K., & Bahniuk, M. H. (1998). Promoting career success through mentoring. *Review of Business, 19*(3), 4–7.

Ibarra, H. (1992). Race, opportunity, and diversity of social circles in managerial networks. *Academy of Management Journal, 38*, 673–703.

Institute, M. (1998). *The new mentoring paradigm* [Internet]. The Mentoring Institute. Retrieved April 15, 2003 from www.mentoring-resources.com/.

Jossi, F. (1997). Mentoring in changing times. *Training and Development, 50*(8), 50–54.

Kelly, S., & Schweitzer, J. H. (1999). Mentoring within a graduate school setting. *College Student Journal, 33*, 130–148.

Kerka, S. (1998). *New perspectives on mentoring* [Internet]. ERIC Digests. Retrieved March 19, 2003, from www.ericfacility.net/ericdigests/ed418249.html.

Leopold, A. (1949). *A sand county almanac.* New York: Oxford University Press.

Levy, J. (1975). *Cesar Chavez: Autobiography of La Causa* (First ed.). New York: W. W. Norton and Company, Inc.

Magdaleno, K. (2004). Lending a helping hand: Mentoring Latina and Latino leaders into the 21st century. Unpublished dissertation, University of California, Los Angeles.

Magdaleno, K. (2009). CALSA: Transforming the power structure. *Leadership, 3*(1), 28–29.

Malone, R. J. (2001). *Principal mentoring.* ERIC Clearinghouse on Educational Management. Retrieved November 11, 2002 from http://eric.uoregon.edu/publications/digests/digest149.html.

Marin, G., & Marin, B. V. (1991). *Research with Hispanic populations* (Vol. 23). Newbury Park, CA: Sage Publications.

Naess, A. (1989). *Ecology, community and lifestyle.* Cambridge, England: Cambridge University Press.

Noe, R. A. (1988). Women and mentoring: A review and research agenda. *Academy of Management Review, 13*, 65–78.

Ostrom, E. S. (1990). *Governing the commons: The evolution of institutions for collective action.* Cambridge, MA: Cambridge University Press.

Pew Hispanic Center tabulations of 2000 Census (5% IPUMS) and 2007 American Community Survey (1% IPUMS).

Powell, G., & Butterfield, A. (1994). Investigating the "glass ceiling" phenomenon: An empirical study of actual promotions to top management. *Academy of Management Journal, 37,* 68–86.

Ragins, B. R., & Cotton, J. (1991). Easier said than done: Gender differences in perceived barriers to gaining a mentor. *Academy of Management Journal, 34,* 939–951.

Reinarz, A. G., & White, E. R. (2001). *Beyond teaching to mentoring: New directions for teaching and learning* (No. 85). San Francisco: Jossey-Bass.

Rosado, C. (1997). The undergirding factor is power: Toward an understanding of prejudice and racism. Retrieved December 31, 2009, from http://curry.edschool. virginia.edu/go/multicultural/papers/caleb/rosado.html.

Samier, E. (2000). Public administration mentorship: Conceptual and pragmatic considerations. *Journal of Educational Administration, 38*(1), 83–101.

Sedlacek, W. E., & Fuertes, J. N. (1993). Barriers to the leadership development of Hispanics in higher education. *NASPA Journal, 30*(4), 277–283.

Sergiovanni, T. J. (1992). *Moral leadership: Getting to the heart of school improvement.* San Francisco: Jossey-Bass, Inc.

Skolimowski, H. (1981). *Eco-Philosophy: Designing new tactics for living.* Salem, MA: Marion Boyars.

Solorzano, D. (1998). Critical race theory, racial and gender microaggressions, and the experiences of Chicana and Chicano scholars. *International Journal of Qualitative Studies in Education 11,* 121–136.

Stoddard, J. T. (1998, March 7). *Croaks from the lily pad: Toward the provision of a peer mentoring program for principals* [Internet]. International Electronic Journal for Leadership in Learning. Retrieved August 20, 2002 from www.acs.ucalgary.ca.

Suarez-Orozco, M. M., & Paez, M. M. (2002). *Latinos remaking America.* London: University of California Press, Ltd.

Swartz, D. (1997). *Culture and power: The sociology of Pierre Bourdieu.* Chicago: The University of Chicago Press, Ltd.

Tannen, D. (1990). *You just don't understand: Men and women in conversation.* New York: William Morrow & Company.

Thomas, D. A. (2001). The truth about mentoring minorities: Race matters. *Harvard Business Review, 79*(4), 98–107.

Wilson, R., & Melendez, S. E. (1988). Strategies for developing minority leadership. In M. F. Green (Ed.), *Leaders for a new era* (pp. 118–136). New York: Macmillan.

Zirkel, S. (2002). Is there a place for me? Role models and academic identity among white students and students of color. *Teachers College Record, 104*(2), 357–376.

Chapter Seven

Leadership for Superintendents Leading Principals

Robert Roelle and Bruce S. Cooper

Successful superintendents can have a positive influence on the performance of principals, who in turn can have a strong impact on classroom
instruction (Marzano et al., 2005). Thus, the importance of the school
principal is unquestionable. Understanding how the leadership practices
of superintendents influence school principals, however, may hold the key
to improving career satisfaction, career longevity, and the effectiveness of
principals as site leaders.

The purpose of this study is to determine the significance of the relationship between superintendents' leadership practices using the *Five
Practices of Exemplary Leadership* defined by Kouzes and Posner
(2008) and principals' job satisfaction, efficacy, and career longevity, as
reported by the principals themselves. With growing demands on school
administrators to prepare children for the challenges of the 21st-century
workforce, the role of the principal is essential and deserves careful
study.

Marzano et al. (2005) claimed that "a highly effective school leader can
have a dramatic influence on the overall academic achievement of students"
(p. 10). In their study of the leadership of school principals, Marzano et al.
found a significant correlation between students' performance and the leadership behaviors of school principals. Years of extensive research have
shown the significance of principal leadership, and in fact, "in many ways
the school principal is the most important and influential individual in any
school" (U.S. Congress, Senate Committee on Equal Educational Opportunity, 1970, p. 56).

RESEARCH QUESTIONS

Existing research demonstrates that despite the significant relationship between both superintendent and principal leadership on positive school climate, safety, and achievement, a major shortage of qualified applicants for the principalship shortage exists (Archer, 2004; Bureau of Labor Statistics, 2008–2009; Copland, 2001; Cushing, Kerrins, & Johnstone, 2003; Grubb & Flessa, 2006; Guterman, 2007; Hinton & Kastner, 2000; Noor, 2008; Norton, 2003; Roza, Celio, Harvey, & Wishon, 2003). However, studies on the relationship between superintendent leadership practices and principals' roles, work, job satisfaction, efficacy, and longevity are limited.

The looming principal shortage begs for more empirical research on how superintendents can use their leadership to improve the overall job outlook of their principals so as to keep good principals in their schools and attract talented new school leaders.

Using Kouzes and Posner's (2008) *Five Practices of Exemplary Leadership*, the following research questions are examined in this study:

1. To what extent do principals feel satisfied with their jobs?
2. What are principals' perceptions of the leadership practices of their superintendents?
3. What specific leadership practices using the Five Practices of their superintendents influence the job satisfaction, efficacy, and longevity of principals?

These questions are answered through an analysis of quantitative data collected on the principals' perceptions of the leadership practices of their superintendents, as well as an evaluation of the general job outlook of the principals.

RESEARCH DESIGN

The relationship between superintendents and principals, who share similar goals for improving student learning experiences for the same children, should be examined further to identify methods to create a collaborative, supportive, and professional partnership, where both superintendent and principal are most productive. The goal of this study is to contribute to the limited research on the impact superintendent leadership practices have on the professional lives of school principals. In light of the imminent principal shortage, finding ways to help principals feel more successful and satisfied with their jobs is critical.

This quantitative research study examines the principal-superintendent relationship through the eyes and experiences of the principal. Using the perceptions of the principal as the focus, this study analyzes the effects of certain leadership practices of the superintendent on the job satisfaction, efficacy, longevity, and career aspirations of principals. The research design is presented in Figure 7.1. Each of the variables is detailed below.

Variables

This study examined three types of variables to attain a full picture of the relationships among the leadership practices of district superintendents; job satisfaction, efficacy, and longevity of school principals; and various demographics. School principals in the sample provided data on each of the variables following the completion of the survey.

Independent Variables: Data were gathered on the background of each principal and their superintendent to see if these demographic variables made any difference—for example, whether their boss, the superintendent, had also

Independent Variables	Intervening Variables	Dependent Variables
Demographics	Leadership Practices of Superintendent (Kouzes& Posner, 2008)	Principal Job Outlook
• Principal Demographics • School Demographics • District Size • Superintendent Experience	• Model the Way • Inspire a Shared Vision • Challenge the Process • Enable Others to Act • Encourage the Heart	• Job Satisfaction • Efficacy • Career Longevity & Aspirations

Figure 7.1.   Design of the Study

served as a principal. Other information included such factors as the principals' gender and age.

Intervening Variables: The intervening variables for this study are the leadership practices of the superintendent as observed and experienced by the school principal. Principals evaluated their superintendent on specific leadership practices as defined by Kouzes and Posner's *Five Practices of Exemplary Leadership* (2008), organized into five categories as follows: *Model the Way, Inspire a Shared Vision, Challenge the Process, Enable Others to Act,* and *Encourage the Heart,* each of which is described below:

1. Model the Way. Leaders should set an example by modeling what they expect others to do. They are clear and confident about their values and principles and clearly express those values and principles to others through words and actions. Leaders continually connect the goals of the organization with their driving values and help others find meaningful ways to work toward those goals (Kouzes & Posner, 2008).

2. Inspire a Shared Vision. Leaders inspire others by painting a picture of what the organization is able to accomplish. They develop a dream for how the values and goals will lead to a better future of the organization, enlisting others in this vision so that it will become their dream as well. They are enthusiastic and committed to making the vision a reality (Kouzes & Posner, 2008).

3. Challenge the Process. Leaders are not afraid to experiment and take risks, even if failure is a possibility. They are committed to positive change and challenge people to try new and innovative methods for solving problems. They understand the difficulties people have with making change but are committed to continuous improvement and advancement of the entire organization (Kouzes & Posner, 2008).

4. Enable Others to Act. Leaders create an environment where change is possible by providing others with the confidence and autonomy to carry out the vision in their own way. They create a trusting, collaborative approach to learning and working, based on powerful relationships among constituents. Leaders inspire others to develop their own leadership abilities and apply them to organizational tasks (Kouzes & Posner, 2008).

5. Encourage the Heart. Effective leaders support people in their organization by continually celebrating and encouraging exemplary behaviors. They find new ways genuinely to thank and recognize people for their dedication and hard work for the organization. Leaders show compassion and understanding for the hardships people face and are flexible when necessary.

They understand that when people care about their work, they are more likely to approach organizational problems as their own (Kouzes & Posner, 2008). Using the *Five Practices of Exemplary Leadership*, this research study seeks to determine the relationship between the leadership practices of super-intendents and the overall job outlook of their principals.

Dependent Variables: In this study, the dependent variables are the percep-tions of principals of their general job satisfaction, a sense of job efficacy, plans for career longevity as a principal, and career aspirations to become a superintendent themselves. Statistical analysis will be used to determine the significance of the relationship between each of the variables in this study, testing the following null hypotheses about the relationship between superin-tendent leadership practices and principal job satisfaction, efficacy, and career longevity.

H1. There is no relationship between the *Model the Way* leadership practices of the superintendent and the job satisfaction, efficacy, and career longevity of the principal.

H2. There is no relationship between the *Inspire a Shared Vision* leadership practices of the superintendent and the job satisfaction, efficacy, and career longevity of the principal.

H3. There is no relationship between the *Challenge the Process* leadership practices of the superintendent and the job satisfaction, efficacy, and career longevity of the principal.

H4. There is no relationship between the *Enable Others to Act* leadership practices of the superintendent and the job satisfaction, efficacy, and career longevity of the principal.

H5. There is no relationship between the *Encourage the Heart* leadership practices of the superintendent and the job satisfaction, efficacy, and career longevity of the principal.

Instrumentation

The *Superintendent Understanding of Principals' Educational Responsibili-ties (SUPER)* survey instrument was developed by the researchers to measure principals' perceptions of their job satisfaction, efficacy, career longevity, and the leadership practices of their superintendent.

The *SUPER* survey has three sections: Section 1 is the *Leadership Practices Inventory-Observer* edition (LPI), developed by researchers and theorists Kouzes and Posner (2003). Permission was granted for the use of their instru-ment in this research. Section 2 contains perception items on the principal's job satisfaction, efficacy, career longevity, and aspirations to become a superinten-dent, and Section 3 gathers demographic information on the participants.

Using the survey, a sampling of principals evaluated their superintendents on the LPI-Observer, a 10-point Likert-scale perceptions survey ranging from

1 = Almost Never to 10 = Almost Always. The LPI-Observer contained 30 different statements, arranged into the following five leadership practice categories: Model the Way, Inspire a Shared Vision, Challenge the Process, Enable Others to Act, and Encourage the Heart.

Principals rated how frequently their superintendent engaged in the behavior described in each statement. Sample items are "sets a personal example of what he/she expects of others," "talks about future trends that will influence how our work gets done," "seeks out challenging opportunities that test his/her own skills and abilities," "develops cooperative relationships among the people that he/she works with," and "praises people for a job well done."

Kouzes and Posner (2002a) developed the LPI after extensive research on *personal best* studies of more than 11,000 surveys, more than 500 interviews, and numerous case studies. Following analysis of their research, Kouzes and Posner (2002a) categorized the practices of leaders into the five categories and developed the LPI. Originally, the LPI had a five-point Likert scale. In 1999 it was changed to "a more robust and sensitive 10-point Likert-scale" (2002b, p. 3), used to measure more accurately leadership values. More than 100,000 surveys are in the LPI database and are used in the continual evaluation of the validity and reliability of the LPI.

Reliability and Validity of the Two Instruments

According to the authors of the LPI, the instrument is statistically valid and reliable. Using Cronbach's alpha, Posner (2008) demonstrated a coefficient range from .84 to .92 for each of the categories and also identified good internal reliability at level .70 and above (see Table 7.1).

The Principal Outlook section of the *SUPER* survey instrument, designed to measure the general job outlook or job satisfaction, efficacy, and career longevity of principals, was developed and tested by the researchers for reliability and validity, separately from the LPI section, for content validity and reliability. A panel of 27 doctoral students and practicing educational administrators familiar with the roles and responsibilities of superintendents and

Table 7.1   Internal Reliability Coefficients (Cronbach's Alpha) of the Leadership Practices Inventory-Observer Edition (LPI): Five Practices of Exemplary Leadership (N = 602,982)

Model the Way	Inspire a Shared Vision	Challenge the Process	Enable Others to Act	Encourage the Heart
.84	.92	.86	.86	.92

Adapted from *The LPI Data Analysis September 2008* by B. Posner, 2008. Retrieved February 1, 2009 from media.wiley.com/assets/1554/74/LPIDataAnalysisSEP08.pdf principals were asked to sort each of the randomly scrambled survey items into three subcategories of job satisfaction, efficacy, and career longevity.

According to Latham and Wexley (1981), an item was considered to have content validity if 80% of the panel members sorted the item into the correct subcategory. Reliability was evident when an item on the survey had a coefficient of 0.70 or higher. Cronbach's alpha was used to test the internal validity of the Principal Outlook section of the *SUPER* instrument. Each of the eight items from the survey was found to have content validity at 80% or higher (see Table 7.2).

Sample

The population for this study was public school principals from a three-county region in New York State. Using electronic survey technology, the *SUPER* survey was sent to 330 principals. Of the 330 principals, 119 (36%) responded to the survey. Individual item *n* values vary because some principals did not respond to one or more survey items in accordance with the terms of the survey consent agreement. The *n* values for each survey item ranged from 112 to 119 and are detailed in the following sections.

FINDINGS

Results of this study are presented in three stages. First, using a t-test, this study compared the differences in how principals rated their superintendents on leadership practices, based on the experiences of their local superintendents as former principals themselves, or not. Next, bivariate correlation analysis was performed to measure the relationships among variables as well as the direction and magnitude of correlations among the leadership practices of the superintendents and the principals' job satisfaction, efficacy, and career longevity and aspirations. Finally, regression analysis was used to determine if combinations of the intervening variables were significant predictors of the job satisfaction of principals.

Table 7.2 Average Agreement among Raters of the Principal Job Outlook Scales of the Superintendent Understanding of Principals' Educational Responsibilities (SUPER) Survey Instrument

Principal Job Outlook Subscale	Number of Items	Average Agreement (%)
Job Satisfaction	3	88
Job Efficacy	3	89
Career Longevity	2	85

Comparison: As shown in Table 7.3, we found significant differences between the principal groups with regard to the leadership practices of their superintendents when comparing principals whose superintendents were former principals with those who never served as principals.

When the superintendent had previously been a principal in the current school district, principals rated their superintendents significantly higher on four of the *Five Practices of Exemplary Leadership*, with the exception of *Enable the Process*. Nevertheless, the mean score for *Enable the Process* was still higher for those superintendents (shown in Column 1, Table 7.3) who worked as principals in their current school district. Experience as a principal in the current school district did not show any significant differences in principal job outlook variables.

BIVARIATE CORRELATION ANALYSIS

At the heart of this study are the correlations between the intervening variables, the *Five Leadership Practices of Exemplary Leadership,* and the dependent variables, the general job outlook of principals. The hypotheses for this study sought to identify the significance of the relationships between superintendents' leadership practices and the job satisfaction, job efficacy, and career longevity and aspirations of principals. The results of the correlation analysis found several highly significant relationships between the intervening and dependent variables, as shown in Table 7.4.

The relationships between principal job satisfaction and each of the *Five Practices of Exemplary Leaders* were highly significant. The same was true

Table 7.3   Results of T-Tests: Intervening Variables by Superintendent's Experience as a Former Principal in Current School District (N = 116)

	Superintendent's Experience as a Former Principal in Current School District					
	Yes (*n* = 18)		No (*n* = 98)			
Variables	*M*	*SD*	*M*	*SD*	*t*	*p*
Intervening Variables—Leadership Practices of Superintendents:						
	Been a Principal in District		*Not Been a Principal in District*			
Model	8.73	1.22	7.60	2.16	3.14	<.01
Inspire	8.71	1.61	7.66	2.36	2.34	.03
Challenge	8.55	1.39	7.41	2.21	2.86	.01
Enable	8.71	1.40	8.19	1.92	1.10	.27
Encourage	8.53	1.63	7.39	2.47	2.49	.02

Table 7.4 Correlation of Principals' Job Outlook (Job Satisfaction, Efficacy, and Job Longevity and Aspirations) with Superintendent's Leadership Practices and Principal's Age

	Principal's Job Outlook		
Variable	Job Satisfaction	Job Efficacy	Career Longevity and Aspirations
Age of Principal and the Five Leadership Practices of Superintendents			
Age	.10	.19*	.23**
Model the Way	.66**	.48**	.13
Inspire a Shared Vision	.63**	.39**	.13
Challenge the Process	.62**	.41**	.16
Enable Others to Act	.64**	.50**	.04
Encourage the Heart	.60**	.36**	.01

*Significant at the p = .05 level (two-tailed). **Significant at the p = .01 level (two-tailed).

when correlating job efficacy of principals and each of the *Five Practices.* Clearly, the leadership of superintendents had an important influence on the job satisfaction and a sense of effectiveness of the principals. The age of a principal also had a significant relationship with job efficacy as well as career longevity and aspirations. The principals age 50 or older felt significantly more effective than younger principals. These same principals were more likely to remain as principals rather than aspire to become superintendents.

The following null hypotheses were tested to determine the significance of the relationships between superintendent leadership practices and principal job satisfaction, efficacy, and career longevity. The results of these tests are explained in the following paragraphs.

Null Hypothesis 1: There is no relationship between the leadership practices of the superintendent in terms of *Model the Way* and job satisfaction, efficacy, and career longevity and aspirations of the principal. As seen in Table 7.4, the variable *Model the Way* had a positive, strong, and highly significant ($p > .001$) correlation with the dependent variable job satisfaction ($r = .66$). *Model the Way* also had a positive, highly significant ($p > .001$), moderate correlation with job efficacy ($r = .48$).

The correlation between *Model the Way* and the dependent variable career longevity was not significant. Therefore, a significant relationship exists between *Model the Way* and principal job satisfaction and job efficacy, but not with career longevity and aspiration. This null hypothesis was rejected for the variables job satisfaction and job efficacy.

Null Hypothesis 2: There is no relationship between the leadership practices of the superintendent in terms of *Inspire a Shared Vision* and job satisfaction, efficacy, and career longevity and aspirations of the principal. The intervening variable *Inspire a Shared Vision* had a positive, highly significant ($p > .001$), strong correlation with the dependent variable job satisfaction ($r = .63$). *Inspire a Shared Vision* also had a positive, highly significant ($p > .001$), moderate correlation with job efficacy ($r = .39$).

The intervening variable *Inspire a Shared Vision* did not have a significant correlational relationship with the dependent variable principal career longevity and aspirations. Therefore, a significant relationship exists between *Inspire a Shared Vision* and principal job satisfaction and job efficacy, but not with career longevity and aspirations. As a result, this null hypothesis was disproved for the variables job satisfaction and job efficacy.

Null Hypothesis 3: There is no relationship between the leadership practices of the superintendent in terms of *Challenge the Process* and job satisfaction, efficacy, and career longevity and aspirations of the principal. The intervening variable *Challenge the Process* had a positive, highly significant ($p > .001$), strong correlation with the dependent variable principal job satisfaction ($r = .62$). *Challenge the Process* also had a positive, highly significant ($p > .001$), moderate correlation with the dependent variable principal job efficacy ($r = .41$).

Once again, *Challenge the Process* did not have a significant correlational relationship with the dependent variable career longevity ($r = .16$). Therefore, a significant relationship exists between *Challenge the Process* and principal job satisfaction and job efficacy, but not with career longevity and aspiration. Consequently, this null hypothesis was disproved for the variables job satisfaction and job efficacy.

Null Hypothesis 4: There is no relationship between the leadership practices of the superintendent in terms of *Enable Others to Act* and job satisfaction, efficacy, and career longevity of the principal. The intervening variable *Enable Others to Act* had a positive, highly significant ($p > .001$), strong correlational relationship with the dependent variable principal job satisfaction ($r = .64$). *Enable Others to Act* also had a positive, highly significant ($p > .001$), moderate correlational relationship with the dependent variable principal job efficacy ($r = .50$).

Enable Others to Act did not have a significant correlational relationship with the dependent variable career longevity ($r = .04$). Therefore, a significant relationship exists between *Enable Others to Act* and principal job satisfaction and job efficacy, but not with career longevity and aspiration. Accordingly, this null hypothesis was disproved for the variables job satisfaction and job efficacy.

Null Hypothesis 5: There is no relationship between the leadership practices of the superintendent in terms of *Encourage the Heart* and job satisfaction, efficacy, and career longevity of the principal. The intervening variable *Encourage the Heart* had a positive, highly significant ($p > .001$), strong correlational relationship with the dependent variable principal job satisfaction ($r = .60$). *Encourage the Heart* also had a positive, highly significant ($p > .001$), moderate correlational relationship with the dependent variable principal job efficacy ($r = .36$).

Encourage the Heart did not have a significant correlational relationship with the dependent variable career longevity ($r = .01$). Thus, a significant relationship exists between *Enable Others to Act* and principal job satisfaction and job efficacy, but not with career longevity and aspiration. Consequently, this null hypothesis was disproved for the variables job satisfaction and job efficacy.

Additional independent variables were also tested for correlational relationships with the dependent variables. As shown in Table 7.4, the only significant relationships existed between the age group of the principals and job efficacy and career longevity of the principals. The age of the principal produced a positive, significant ($p = .04$), but fairly weak correlation with job efficacy of the principals ($r = .19$). In addition, age group of principals had the only positive, significant ($p = .01$) correlation with the career longevity of the principals ($r = .23$).

REGRESSION ANALYSIS: PREDICTING JOB SATISFACTION

A series of regression analyses were conducted to determine which, if any, intervening variables together were good predictors of job satisfaction, job efficacy, or career longevity and aspirations.

The regression analysis determined that variables best predict principal job satisfaction. As seen in Table 7.5, two variables were good predictors of job satisfaction. *Model the Way* leadership practices of superintendents were the strongest predictors of principal job satisfaction. The second significant predictor of job satisfaction was the job efficacy of the principal. Together, highly rated superintendent *Model the Way* behaviors and principal job efficacy ratings explained 63% of the variance in principals' job satisfaction and were significant at the $p = < .000$ level.

Table 7.5   Regression Analysis: Variables Best Predicting Principals' Job Satisfaction (N = 119)

Variable	B	SE B	BFTA	F value	p
Model	0.12	0.02	0.46	36.86	< .001
Job Efficacy	0.59	0.10	0.45	36.08	< .001

$R = 0.796$; $R^2 = 0.634$; *Adj.* $R^2 = 0.626$; $df = 90$; $SE = 0.341$; *F-ratio* = 76.324

IMPLICATIONS

The findings of this study provide important information for school leaders as well as baseline data for future research on how leadership influences principals' job outlook. As superintendents struggle to find ways to solve the mystery of the leadership gap at the school level, they should begin by looking in the mirror. The results of this study demonstrate that the leadership of the superintendent is not only important for improving student achievement but also critical for improving the overall job outlook for their principals.

Superintendents should focus their attention on improving their abilities to provide leadership to principals in accordance with the Kouzes and Posner (2008) model for leadership: *Model the Way, Inspire a Shared Vision, Challenge the Process, Enable Others to Act,* and *Encourage the Heart.* Each of these leadership practices was found to improve significantly the job satisfaction of principals and the general feelings of effectiveness of principals. Judging by past research that identifies the principal as the most important leader at the school level and the results of this study, superintendents should spend time examining their own leadership practices to see how they can be improved to meet the needs of principals in their districts.

Since superintendents influence student performance indirectly, how they lead their principals is most important. Superintendents can have a greater influence on students if they can learn to improve their leadership of their principals. Self-evaluation, reflection, and improvement of superintendent leadership will improve the job satisfaction and efficacy of principals.

The results of this study confirm and enhance some of the current research on the necessity of quality superintendent leadership for the success of school principals. Each of the *Five Practices of Exemplary Leadership* was found to have significant correlations with principals' job satisfaction and job efficacy. The following paragraphs link these findings to current research on the relationship between superintendents and principals.

MODEL THE WAY

"People first follow the person, then the plan" (Kouzes & Posner, 2002a, p. 15). Our study found a highly significant relationship between the job satisfaction and job efficacy of principals and the *Model the Way* leadership practices of their superintendents. Kouzes and Posner (2008) identified modeling as a very important characteristic of a leader, in which leaders are able to articulate their values to others by behaving exactly as they would have others behave.

Furthermore, Lee (2005) found that principals valued having shared goals with their superintendents—determining that when superintendents demonstrate a commitment to student achievement, principals and superintendents can have a "symbiotic relationship" as they work together toward the same goals. In accordance with the findings of this study, superintendents should be willing to demonstrate a full commitment to their vision by becoming an active participant.

INSPIRE A SHARED VISION

Cudeiro (2005) found that successful superintendents were committed to enlisting their principals in a shared vision by providing clear and specific goals to focus on student learning. These superintendents established the primary responsibility of principals as instructional leaders and translated their vision to principals continually through written and verbal communications. Kouzes and Posner (2008) postulated *Inspire a Shared Vision* as one of the *Five Practices of Exemplary Leadership*.

The results of this study demonstrated a highly significant relationship between principal job satisfaction and efficacy and the leadership practice of superintendents to *Inspire a Shared Vision*. With the results of this study in mind, superintendents should dedicate time and energy to developing a clear vision for their principals and seek to promote the vision so that others adopt it as their own.

CHALLENGE THE PROCESS

Kouzes and Posner (2008) claimed that effective leaders are willing to take risks to find the latest and most innovative ways to meet the challenges of an organization. This study found a highly significant correlation between principals' job satisfaction and efficacy and the superintendents' ability to *Challenge the Process*. According to the principals in this study, their superintendents were good at seeking out interesting opportunities, challenging others to discover new and innovative solutions, looking outside the normal scope of the profession to find solutions, learning from mistakes, and being willing to take risks despite possible failure.

West and Derrington (2009) noted that principals in their study were confident they could find new and innovative ways to solve problems because they were empowered to do so by their superintendents. If principals made mistakes, they knew they would not be penalized. Together, the superintendents and principals worked toward finding solutions. These superintendents challenged their principals to take calculated risks, thus creating a secure environment where creativity and innovation were fostered and encouraged.

ENABLE OTHERS TO ACT

Waters and Marzano (2005) identified successful superintendents as those who provided their principals with a defined autonomy or freedom to do their jobs in their own way within reasonable parameters. Burbach and Butler (2005) and Lee (2005) also identified autonomy and the lack of superintendent micromanagement as important factors for principals' success and efficacy. In our study, principals rated their superintendents as very strong at *Enable Others to Act* practices, in which the superintendents create an environment where principals can make their own decisions and take ownership of both the successes and failures of the decisions they make.

Principals' job satisfaction and job efficacy were highly influenced by the superintendent's ability to enable them to act as postulated by Kouzes and Poser (2008), as well as Waters and Marzano, Burbach and Butler, and Lee. Clearly, providing principal autonomy is important and superintendents should find ways to continue to empower principals to practice their own leadership.

ENCOURAGE THE HEART

Past research on the principal-superintendent relationship repeated the word "trust" over and over again. Burbach and Butler (2005), Lee (2005), and Shivers (1999) all cited trust as one of the most important elements needed to develop a productive relationship between the principal and superintendent. Shivers claimed that having a strong, personal relationship with his superintendent was most important in performing his duties well as a principal. He identified *trust* as the first in his seven factors affecting the relationship between superintendents and principals. Shivers claimed that *little things,* such as dropping a note or making a phone call to affirm a job well done, were important elements in developing this relationship.

Burbach and Butler (2005) claimed that trust and appreciation were very important factors in developing a positive relationship between the principal and superintendent. The results of our study confirmed the importance of the superintendents' ability to *Encourage the Hearts* of their principals. Kouzes and Posner (2008) claimed that leaders must work to develop positive relationships with people by developing trust and continually celebrating the hard work they do.

Superintendents, therefore, should spend more time developing relationships with their principals and finding ways to express their appreciation of the stressful work principals do. This recognition may be one of the most pivotal factors in keeping good principals on the job and attracting new leaders to this challenging role.

RECOMMENDATIONS FOR RESEARCH AND PRACTICE

The results of this study demonstrated several interesting and significant findings related to the leadership practices of superintendents, the importance of superintendent experience as a former principal, and the overall job satisfaction and efficacy of principals. The following are recommendations for future research and best practices based on these findings.

1. Conduct research on the relationship between the leadership practices of other central office personnel and the job satisfaction and efficacy of principals. In many school districts other key administrators may influence the performance of principals. Larger school districts, in particular, employ various administrators, such as assistant superintendents, department leaders, and directors. In some school districts, these midlevel administrators are responsible for supporting and supervising principals. In a number of cases, these educational leaders may have more influence on the job satisfaction and efficacy of the principals whom they lead than the superintendent.

Research on how the leadership of other central office personnel influences the general job outlook of principals would provide another perspective on how to improve the job satisfaction, job efficacy, and career aspirations of school principals.

2. Perform 360-degree evaluation of superintendent leadership. A method for improving the leadership practices of superintendents would be to conduct frequent, localized self-studies among superintendents and their principals using Kouzes and Posner's (2008) *Five Practices of Exemplary Leadership.* In such a study, superintendents would evaluate their own leadership practices and then have their principals reflect on the leadership practices of the superintendent, thus providing superintendents with data from their own staff on how they are performing as leaders. Superintendents would then be able to see if their own perceptions of their leadership practices are consistent with their principals' evaluations.

3. Involve superintendents in professional development on the Five Practices of Exemplary Leadership. Following the completion of a self-study, superintendents should have a more accurate idea of which leadership practices they need to improve. One should not necessarily assume that all superintendents would be good at improving their leadership practices, especially in areas where they are lacking them. Like all other professionals, superintendents need ongoing development to learn new practices and abandon poor leadership habits.

States, counties, local school boards, professional superintendent associations, or even principal associations should establish professional development programs to track the superintendent from the commencement of the perception study (from recommendation 1) to analysis of the data to a professional development program targeted to the areas in need of improvement.

These programs should be practical, work within the superintendents' busy schedules, and focus on implementation strategies. Although sometimes a difficult task, superintendent development would be useful in creating an environment where principals can feel better about their jobs. Ultimately, principals who can do their jobs better will likely have students who perform better.

4. Provide principals with mentoring opportunities from current or former principals. Cudeiro (2005) found in her research that one of the best ways superintendents were successful in supporting their new principals was to provide them with a mentor. Just as new teachers often need mentoring, new principals should be afforded the same opportunity.

Principal mentors could be experienced, practicing principals or former principals or even superintendents who were very successful in their leadership roles in their careers. These mentors could be invaluable to new principals who are learning how to handle the day-to-day issues of their schools; moreover, they could provide guidance for handling the most challenging situations that often occur unexpectedly.

These mentor principals could be formally assigned, paid a stipend, and evaluated on their mentoring to establish their efforts as an official duty or job. In larger districts a senior administrative position could be created, employing a successful principal or possibly a retired principal, who would focus specifically on the support and development of new principals. Smaller districts should partner with other school districts to create the same position.

5. Give new superintendents mentoring opportunities from successful colleagues. Just as principals need mentors, superintendents would also benefit from the formal support, development, and guidance from an experienced and successful leader. In schools where principals are desperately in need of leadership, new superintendents may not have the luxury of time to learn how to become good leaders. Mentors could help new superintendents support their principals while they develop their own leadership. Former superintendents are often looking for part-time work to continue their practice during retirement.

State or local superintendent or principal organizations should recruit and train a group of superintendent mentors who can help superintendents improve their leadership practices as outlined by Kouzes and Posner (2008). These mentors could provide superintendents with the critical but nonevaluative eye needed to help them improve their practices.

6. *Allow principals to work with more autonomy.* Kouzes and Posner (2008) claimed that good leaders *Enable Others to Act.* The results from this study, together with the findings of Waters and Marzano (2005), Burbach and Butler (2005) and Lee (2005), confirmed that principals need the autonomy and authority to make their own decisions.

As difficult as this may be, superintendents should provide principals with the ability to do their jobs without the pressures from being a micromanager. Superintendents will need to become skilled at knowing when to give their principals autonomy and when to intervene or give more support. This research clearly shows that autonomy should not be overlooked or underestimated in building leadership at the building and district levels.

7. *Provide principals with more professional support staff.* If superintendents intend to make the job of principal more attractive and desirable for the next generation of education leaders, they should find ways to help principals do their jobs. Past research has shown that principals often find themselves drowning in the management of school-related activities, which keeps them from becoming effective leaders for their teachers (Copland, 2001; Cudeiro, 2005; Grubb & Flessa, 2006; Portin & Shen, 2005)

In our study, one of the strongest correlations was found between superintendents' *Enable Others to Act* behaviors and principals' job satisfaction and job efficacy. Clearly, superintendents should foster an environment where their principals have the resources and the staffing necessary to practice their own leadership. If principals are expected to be leaders of the teachers, these school leaders need to be freed from some other managerial tasks that consume their time and drain their energy.

To free up time for principals and allow them to focus on their own leadership practices, school districts need to assign more staff to manage these nonleadership duties. First, school districts should listen to principals to find out what they need, including perhaps an additional clerical worker to assist with phone calls and paperwork, such as compliance documents and scheduling forms. In other cases, the principal may need an assistant principal to help support teachers or a dean of students to manage some of the discipline issues.

Other principals may require more instructional support staff, such as professional developers or even subject-specific supervisors. These recommendations, however, are not meant to create more supervision and control of principals, as is sometimes the case when assistant superintendents are hired. The purpose of the additional staff should be to provide principals with the support and flexibility they need to better lead their staffs.

8. Recognize talent from within the organization. One of the key findings in this study was that principals felt their superintendent was a better leader if he or she had once been a principal within the same school district. Insider superintendents were rated significantly higher on their leadership practices than those superintendents who did not have experience as a principal in the same school district. These superintendents were better at the leadership practices of *Model the Way, Inspire a Shared Vision, Challenge the Process,* and *Encourage the Heart.*

Boards of education should consider these findings when looking to fill vacancies created by departing superintendents. New superintendents, hired from within the same school district, may be more likely to understand the initiatives, the staff, the students, and the culture of both the school system and the community. Insider superintendents clearly have an advantage over outside-the-district superintendents when it comes to providing leadership to principals.

These findings should not be overlooked (Carlson, 1971). Finding a superintendent who can positively influence the job satisfaction and efficacy of their principals could be extremely valuable.

9. Develop a clear vision and model desired behaviors. The highest correlation found in this study was between superintendents who exhibited *Model the Way* behaviors and the job satisfaction of their principals. Essentially, superintendents who modeled desired behaviors were very likely to have principals with high levels of job satisfaction. Kouzes and Posner (2008) claimed that leaders who have a clear vision and express their values to others through words and actions are seen as more credible and promote greater organizational loyalty.

When leaders are clear about what they believe and then do what they say they will do, their constituents respect them. As affirmed by this study, superintendents who model the way have principals with a greater sense of job satisfaction and job efficacy.

CONCLUSION

This study provides important information for school leaders as well as baseline data for future research on how leadership influences principal job outlook. As superintendents struggle to find ways to solve the mystery of the leadership gap at the school level, they should begin by looking to themselves and at their own attitudes and practices. The results of this study demonstrate that the leadership of the superintendent is not only important for improving student achievement but also for improving the overall job outlook for their principals.

Superintendents should focus their attention on improving their abilities to provide leadership to principals in accordance with Kouzes and Posner's (2008) model for leadership: *Model the Way, Inspire a Shared Vision, Challenge the Process, Enable Others to Act,* and *Encourage the Heart.* Each of these leadership practices was found to significantly improve the job satisfaction and the general feelings of effectiveness of principals.

Judging by past research that identifies the principal as the most important leader at the school level and the results of this study, superintendents need to spend more time looking at their own leadership practices to help meet the needs of principals. Since superintendents influence student performance indirectly, we see that working with their principals is most important. Superintendents can have a greater influence on students if they can learn to improve their leadership of their principals. Self-evaluation, reflection, and improvement of superintendent leadership should help to improve the job satisfaction and effectiveness of their school principals.

REFERENCES

Archer, J. (2004, September 15). Tackling an impossible job. *Education Week, 24*(3), S1-S7. Retrieved February 9, 2009 from Professional Development Collection database.

Burbach, H., & Butler, A. (2005). Turnaround principals. *School Administrator, 62*(6), 24–31.

Bureau of Labor Statistics. (2008–2009). *U.S. Department of Labor, Occupational Outlook Handbook, 2008–09 Edition, Education Administrators.* Retrieved February 19, 2009 from www.bls.gov/oco/ocos007.htm

Carlson, R. O. (1971*). Executive succession and organizational change: Place-bound and career-bound superintendents of schools.* Chicago: University of Chicago, Midwest Administrator Center. Read more: www.faqs.org/copyright/executive-succession-and-organizational-change-place-bound/#ixzz0WzPEufZ2.

Copland, M. (2001). The myth of the super-principal. *Phi Delta Kappan, 82*, 528–533.

Cudeiro, A. (2005). Leading student achievement: A study finds superintendents affecting instructional gains through their strong relationships with principals. *School Administrator, 62*(11), 16.

Cushing, K. S., Kerrins, J. A., & Johnstone, T. (2003). Disappearing principals: What is the real reason behind the shortage of applications for principal positions across the state and nation? It's the job, stupid! *Leadership, 32*(5), 28–29, 37.

Grubb, N., & Flessa, J. (2006). A job too big for one: Multiple principals and other nontraditional approaches to school leadership. *Educational Administration Quarterly, 42*(4), 518–550.

Guterman, J. (2007). *Where have all the principals gone?* Retrieved February 10, 2009 from the George Lucas Education Foundation website: www.edutopia.org/where-have-all-principals-gone.

Hinton, L., & Kastner, J, (2000). *Vermont principal shortage. Vermont Legislative Research Shop*. Retrieved January 25, 2009 from www.uvm.edu/~vlrs/doc/vermonts_principal_shortage.htm

Kouzes, J., & Posner, B. (2002a). *The leadership challenge* (3rd ed.). San Francisco: John Wiley & Sons, Inc.

Kouzes, J., & Posner, B. (2002b). *The leadership practices inventory: Theory and evidence behind the five practices of exemplary leadership*. Retrieved January 21, 2009 from http://media.wiley.com/assets/463/74/lc_jb_appendix.pdf.

Kouzes, J., & Posner, B. (2003). *The leadership practices inventory-Observer survey instrument*. San Francisco: John Wiley & Sons.

Kouzes, J., & Posner, B. (2008). The *leadership challenge* (4th ed.) [electronic version]. San Francisco: Jossey-Bass. Accessed online at Books24x7.

Latham, G. P., & Wexley, K. N. (1981). *Increasing productivity through performance appraisal*. Reading, MA: Addison-Wesley Publishing Company.

Lee, J. W. (2005). *A study of principal-superintendent partnerships*. Unpublished doctoral dissertation, New York University, New York. Retrieved February 23, 2009 from Dissertations & Theses: Full Text database (Publication No. AAT 3166534).

Marzano, R., Waters, T., & McNulty, B. (2005). *School leadership that works: From research to results*. Alexandria, VA: ASCD.

Noor, M. (2008, August 3). Shortage of principals is feared as a wave of retirements looms. [Electronic version.] *New York Times*. Retrieved February 19, 2009 from www.nytimes.com/2008/08/03/nyregion/nyregionspecial2/03principalsct.html.

Norton, M. (2003). Let's keep our quality school principals on the job. *The High School Journal, 86*(2), 50–56.

Portin, B., & Shen, J. (2005). The changing principalship. In J. Shen (Ed.), *School principals* (pp. 179–200). New York: Peter Lang Publishing.

Posner, B. (2008). *The LPI Data Analysis September 2008*. Santa Clara University. Retrieved February 1, 2009 from http://media.wileycom/ssets/1554/74/LPI-DataAnalysisSEP08.pdf

Roza, M., Celio, M., Harvey, J., & Wishon, S. (2003). *A matter of definition: Is there truly a shortage of school principals?* (ERIC Document Reproduction Service No. ED477647). Retrieved February 19, 2009 from ERIC database.

Shivers, J. (1999). Seven factors affecting the relationship between superintendent and principals. In R. Van Der Bogart & S. Boris-Schacter (Eds.), *The changing relationship between principal and superintendent* (pp. 43–52). San Francisco: Jossey-Bass.

U.S. Congress, Senate Committee on Equal Educational Opportunity. (1970). *Toward equal educational opportunity*. Washington, DC: Government Printing Office.

Waters, T., & Marzano, R. (2005). School district leadership that works: The effect of superintendent leadership on student achievement. A working paper. *Mid-Continent Research for Education and Learning (McREL)*, (ERIC Document Reproduction Service No. ED494270). Retrieved November 27, 2007 from ERIC database.

West, C., & Derrington, M. (2009). *Leadership teaming: The superintendent-principal relationship*. Thousand Oaks, CA: Corwin Press.

Epilogue

Retaining and Sustaining the Best in a Dynamic Environment

Rick Ginsberg

The end of the story is always the hardest to write. But it is really the most important part. In a novel, the end ties together all that has come before, usually in a profound way that may be thought-provoking, heart wrenching, or in the case of a mystery, just plain exciting. In research, the ending strives to derive some meaning from all the data presented. This book's editors began with the simple admonition that school and district leadership roles were never easy. But given the circumstances today, many leaders are just giving up. In their words, they are "crashing and leaving their posts."

The chapters in this book leave us with a story that isn't necessarily new, but it is a time where the dynamics are such that they are more uncertain than ever in the past. The challenges facing today's schools seem to be growing exponentially. Given the changing demographics, increasing accountability demands, and fiscal and other constraints that school leaders are dealing with, the need mounts for better, practical ways to retain and sustain the right individuals for leadership roles. As several of the chapters in this book imply, the task in many instances is daunting.

The book does suggest both reasons for optimism and some challenges ahead regarding matters related to the future health of the key leadership roles in K–12 education. On the positive side, this book's chapters present interesting and in some instances novel ideas for enhancing leadership retention and sustainability in schools. The chapter by Ernestine K. Enomoto, for example, focuses on the need for socializing assistant principals into their roles as school leaders. A call for better planning for leadership succession and sustaining professional development for leaders in rural schools is emphasized.

The Sharon Conley and Margaret Christensen Chapter 3 identifies the creation and nurturing of high-functioning administrative teams as a means of making administrative work roles more attractive in terms of psychological and work engagement. They conclude that "administrative teams that engage their members seem likely to increase member effectiveness as well as to create an atmosphere conducive of career leadership positions."

My Chapter 4 with Karen D. Multon examines the emotional side of leading during a period of financial stress. We found that many principals displayed an uncanny ability to navigate the difficult economic times by maintaining a "can-do" attitude, taking time carefully to plan, being transparent in their ongoing communications, and making certain to take care of themselves, no matter how intense the circumstances.

Sharon Conley, Terrence E. Deal, and Ernestine K. Enomoto, in Chapter 5, examine the difficulty of changing routines and rituals and offer sage advice for leaders undertaking changes that affect these regularities in the work setting. Change efforts in the past, they argue, have largely ignored "the training and the intangible aspects of schools that make any organization thrive."

The Chapter 6 by Kenneth R. Magdaleno examines the need for the mentoring of Latino and Latina school administrators. Especially given the changing public school demographic picture in the country, he underscores the significance of mentoring for this subset of the K–12 leadership population, heightened by the idiosyncratic issues they confront in leadership roles and the "value of mentoring in a long-range career developmental view."

Finally, Robert Roelle and Bruce S. Cooper, in Chapter 7, examine the relationship of superintendent leadership to principal satisfaction and feelings of efficacy. Using Kouzes and Posner's (2008) five practices of exemplary leadership as a guide, they identify key practices that superintendents should employ to bolster the success of their district's principals.

The seven chapters, therefore, point to concrete ideas and potential practices for supporting principals and principal succession at a time when recruiting and retaining school leaders is problematic. But the news isn't all so rosy. The chapters also suggest several themes that characterize the role of principal that may undermine any attempts at supporting leadership in the field.

Ernestine K. Enomoto's chapter on assistant principal socialization indicated that training and support are not always top priorities for the administrators in leadership roles in school districts. Many induction experiences are characterized as "sink or swim" for new leaders. Research is cited that principals often feel abandoned when first on the job. The theme—that training and support are not necessarily a priority—is prevalent in many of the chapters in the book. Part of the socialization into a principalship appears to be:

you are on your own! As Enomoto illustrates, professional development is "less consistent than desirable to sustain new administrators in remote school settings."

A consistent theme in this book is the need for careful strategizing for helping principals to be successful, including more poignant professional development, carefully designed mentoring, supportive work teams, appreciating the power of routines and rituals, finding balance in one's life, and a variety of other useful ideas. As Conley, Deal, and Enomoto imply, principals really need to be trained to deal with promoting changes that undermine the regularities of leaders' work. In today's atmosphere of increasing accountability and fewer resources, the importance of such training cannot be overemphasized.

Another theme is the systemic view needed to capture the reality of principal work in schools. The Roelle and Cooper chapter underscores how superintendents are important for principals' satisfaction and feelings of efficacy. In a system, all parts are interrelated. Similarly, the Ginsberg and Multon chapter underscores how spending cuts to schools affect students, highlighting the interconnectivity of all functions of a school from the perspective of the principal's office. Thus, principal support cannot be viewed in isolation, but rather must be understood in the context of the entire system. Strategies for support must be carefully coupled with the varying components of the school organization.

Finally, the difficulty of school leadership jobs was a theme characteristic of all the chapters. In Magdaleno's chapter on Latina and Latino principal mentoring, the racism that these leaders face calls for a special sort of mentoring to help them successfully navigate the issues they will confront. The Ginsberg and Multon chapter focused on the *tornadoes of negativity* that the principals were confronting, while at the same time having to meet accountability demands, despite the loss of needed support resources. Assistant principals were depicted in the Enomoto chapter as often too busy to attend their own support workshops; they were too occupied to do the required observations, and the very leaders who established the program often were unable to attend due to other time pressures.

Other examples could be drawn from the book's chapters, but the point is clear. Being a principal, assistant principal, and superintendent is a difficult and demanding position, and the work itself can somehow undermine attempts at providing support for leaders on the job.

What we are left with—what our ending has to be—is a simple set of questions. Will the field take the good ideas presented throughout this book, and in conjunction with other practices, strive to move the field forward to support retaining and sustaining principals? Will these efforts become a priority? Or will the difficulties and realities that emerge as themes from this book over-come attempts to make progress? As leadership positions in schools continue to come open and remain open, the future of our schools may rest with how these questions are answered.

REFERENCES

Kouzes, J., & Posner, B. (2008). *The leadership challenge* (4th ed.) [electronic version]. San Francisco: Jossey-Bass.

Notes

NOTES TO CHAPTER 3

1. Respondents indicated that they met formally with other team members as follows: one or fewer (4.2%), two (29.2%), three (13.9%), four (48.6%), or five or more (4.2%) times per month.

2. Caution should be exercised in interpreting the factor analysis owing to a small sample size. The factor analysis was conducted with a principal component analysis, with a varimax rotation. Only factors with loadings above .50 are included in scale construction.

3. We included in our regression equations: first, the variables related to design features, organizational support, and task and interpersonal process that were significant correlates of each outcome and, in our second regression analysis, the enabling conditions that were significant correlates. Significant predictors from these regressions were then used to run final models.

NOTES TO CHAPTER 5

1. Names are in alphabetical order and do not reflect differential contributions. We appreciate Justin Smith's comments on earlier versions of this chapter.

About the Contributors

Sharon Conley, Ph.D., is professor of education in the Gevirtz Graduate School of Education at University of California, Santa Barbara. Her latest articles include "Organizational Routines in Flux: A Case Study of Change in Recording and Monitoring Student Attendance" with Ernestine K. Enomoto in *Education and Urban Society* and "Teacher Role Stress, Satisfaction, Commitment and Intentions to Leave: A Structural Model" in *Psychological Reports.*

Bruce S. Cooper, Ph.D., is professor of educational leadership and policy at Fordham University Graduate School of Education in New York City. His latest books as editor and author include *Handbook on Education Politics and Policy* with James Cibulka and Lance Fusarelli (Routledge Press) and *The Rising State: How State Power Is Transforming Our Nation's Schools* (SUNY Press) with Bonnie Fusarelli. He is former president of the Politics of Education and a recent recipient of the Jay D. Scribner Award for Mentoring from the University Council of Education Administration.

Margaret Christensen, Ph.D., is assistant superintendent–human resources and director of professional learning in the Green Bay, Wisconsin, Public School District.

Terrence E. Deal, Ph.D., is formerly Irving R. Melbo Professor at the Rossier School of Education at the University of Southern California and resides in San Luis Obispo, California.

Ernestine K. Enomoto, Ed.D., is professor in the Department of Educational Administration at University of Hawaii at Manoa.

Rick Ginsberg, Ph.D., is dean of the School of Education and professor in the Department of Educational Leadership and Policy Studies at the University of Kansas.

Kenneth R. Magdaleno, Ed.D., is an associate professor in the Department of Educational Research and Administration at the Kremen School of Education and Human Development at California State University, Fresno.

Karen D. Multon, Ph.D., is professor and chair of the Department of Psychology and Research in Education in the School of Education at the University of Kansas.

Robert Roelle, Ed.D., is principal of Prospect Hill Elementary School in Westchester County, New York, and a graduate of Fordham University.

Michelle D. Young, Ph.D., is the executive director of the University Council for Educational Administration (UCEA) and an associate professor in educational leadership and policy at the University of Texas.